The Strategy
of Social Regulation

Studies in the Regulation of Economic Activity

The Strategy
of Social Regulation:
Decision Frameworks
for Policy

LESTER B. LAVE

The Brookings Institution/Washington, D.C.

Library of Congress Cataloging in Publication Data:
Lave, Lester B.
  The strategy of social regulation.
  (Studies in the regulation of economic
activity)
  Bibliography: p.
  Includes index.
1. Industry and state—United States. 2. Trade
regulation—United States. 3. Consumer
protection—United States. 4. Environmental
policy—United States. I. Title. II. Title:
Social regulation. III. Series.
HD3616.U47L37   338.973
ISBN 0-8157-5162-1   81-7685
ISBN 0-8157-5161-3 (pbk.)   AACR2

9 8 7 6 5 4 3 2

THE BROOKINGS INSTITUTION is an independent organization devoted to nonpartisan research, education, and publication in economics, government, foreign policy, and the social sciences generally. Its principal purposes are to aid in the development of sound public policies and to promote public understanding of issues of national importance.

The Institution was founded on December 8, 1927, to merge the activities of the Institute for Government Research, founded in 1916, the Institute of Economics, founded in 1922, and the Robert Brookings Graduate School of Economics and Government, founded in 1924.

The Board of Trustees is responsible for the general administration of the Institution, while the immediate direction of the policies, program, and staff is vested in the President, assisted by an advisory committee of the officers and staff. The by-laws of the Institution state: "It is the function of the Trustees to make possible the conduct of scientific research, and publication, under the most favorable conditions, and to safeguard the independence of the research staff in the pursuit of their studies and in the publication of the results of such studies. It is not a part of their function to determine, control, or influence the conduct of particular investigations or the conclusions reached."

The President bears final responsibility for the decision to publish a manuscript as a Brookings book. In reaching his judgment on the competence, accuracy, and objectivity of each study, the President is advised by the director of the appropriate research program and weighs the views of a panel of expert outside readers who report to him in confidence on the quality of the work. Publication of a work signifies that it is deemed a competent treatment worthy of public consideration but does not imply endorsement of conclusions or recommendations.

The Institution maintains its position of neutrality on issues of public policy in order to safeguard the intellectual freedom of the staff. Hence interpretations or conclusions in Brookings publications should be understood to be solely those of the authors and should not be attributed to the Institution, to its trustees, officers, or other staff members, or to the organizations that support its research.

Foreword

In 1978 the author of this book was asked to assist President Carter's economic and science advisers in formulating proposals for further amending the Federal Food and Drug Act of 1906 so as to deal with difficult issues in the regulation of saccharin and sodium nitrite. In the past decade Congress, seeming to prefer ad hoc solutions to such problems, tended to pass special legislation whenever an executive agency promulgated regulations that appeared to be against the public interest. For example, in 1977 Congress prevented the Food and Drug Administration from banning saccharin for eighteen months while the National Academy of Sciences studied the issue. After the eighteen-month period elapsed without any clear recommendation from the Academy, Congress was presented with an apparently irreconcilable conflict in balancing public desire for a nonnutritive sweetener against the risk of unnecessary exposure to carcinogens. A White House interagency working group devoted to assessing the health dangers of food additives was unable to come up with a solution that would satisfy the Department of Health, Education, and Welfare, and hence systematic reform was put aside.

The generic issue exemplified by the saccharin episode is whether the costs, risks, and benefits of proposed food regulations—and of health and safety regulations generally—can be estimated with enough accuracy and reliability to become an important basis for regulatory decisionmaking. The costs and benefits of economic regulation can doubtless be estimated, although the estimates vary greatly with differing but equally realistic assumptions. Moreover, because health and safety regulations are fraught with uncertainty and emotion, systematic quantitative analysis will not necessarily improve the quality of regulatory decisions.

This book is an examination of the contribution that quantitative analysis has made and can make to regulatory decisions concerning health and safety. In arguing that careful analysis can enlighten regulatory decisions, the author also shows that Congress has written into various regulatory statutes a set of "decision frameworks" that preclude considering—or allow only indirect consideration of—analytical results. Thus while the methods and analysis presented here may be of immediate use to some regulatory agencies, other agencies cannot use them without a change in their enabling legislation.

Lester Lave is a senior fellow in the Brookings Economic Studies program. He is indebted to Robert Mendelsohn, Albert Nichols, Michael Gough, and Richard Merrill, who read the entire manuscript in its penultimate draft and offered many insightful comments. He is also grateful to Susan L. Woollen and Valerie J. Harris, who typed the manuscript, and to Elizabeth Callison and Lewis Alexander, who provided research assistance and, under the supervision of Penelope Harpold, verified its factual content. The manuscript was edited by Tadd Fisher; the index was prepared by Patricia Foreman.

This is the fifteenth publication in the Brookings series of Studies in the Regulation of Economic Activity. The series is devoted to presenting the results of research focused on public policies toward business. Initial funds for the research on which this book is based were provided by the Council on Wage and Price Stability. Most of the financial support for the project as a whole was provided by grants from the Ford Foundation, the Alfred P. Sloan Foundation, and the Alex C. Walker Foundation.

The views presented here are those of the author and should not be ascribed to the persons or organizations whose assistance is acknowledged above, or to the trustees, officers, or other staff members of the Brookings Institution.

BRUCE K. MAC LAURY
President

May 1981
Washington, D.C.

Contents

CHAPTER ONE

Social Regulation: Cure or Problem?

BEGINNING in the mid-1960s the public perceived health, safety, and environmental problems as important, worthy of attention, and requiring new institutions.[1] Congress enacted a set of laws that were qualitatively different from previous regulations in giving wide power and responsibility to newly created social regulatory agencies. The nation embraced this reform movement without comprehensive ideas of its costs, the best way to proceed, or the disruption it could cause. An important problem had prompted general agreement that something should be done; it was the American way to begin immediately and to figure out the details as things went along.

The Problem

A decade and a half after the beginning of this social regulation, it is evident that all is not well. Each of the regulatory agencies has become embroiled in controversy. Their regulations are assailed as impeding innovation and damaging the health of the economy in general and of small businesses in particular. Implementation of the rules is alleged to favor

1. In 1965, 17 percent of those surveyed in a Gallup poll regarded "reducing pollution of air and water" as one of the three most important problems requiring the government's attention; by April 1970, 53 percent of those surveyed chose air and water pollution, placing it second only to "reducing the amount of crime," and that by only three percentage points. Since then the surveys have indicated that Americans attribute slightly less importance to environmental problems, but the category still ranks in the top half dozen in importance. See Robert Cameron Mitchell, "Silent Spring/Solid Majorities," pp. 16–17; and Lester B. Lave, "Health, Safety, and Environmental Regulations," pp. 135–37.

1

certain groups, to be ineffective, and to impose unnecessarily large costs on the economy.[2]

An unlikely coalition of businessmen, labor unions, and some counties and states are attempting to sweep aside these social regulations by delaying implementation, requiring legislative or judicial review of the regulations, or even repealing the laws. Opinion polls, however, indicate that a majority of the public supports the goals of social regulation and that this support has eroded very little since 1970.[3] Thus significant relaxation of the goals seems unlikely. While delaying implementation of regulations, paralyzing a regulatory agency, or even repealing some laws is possible, the result is likely to be public frustration because environmental goals are not being achieved and, consequently, the enactment of even more stringent laws. The nation has a Hobbesian choice: Americans cannot live with regulation and do not want to live without it.

The Solution

The high cost of social regulation arose because of the public's unrealistic expectations concerning what could be accomplished by such regulation, as well as the failure of Congress and the regulators to appreciate its limitations.[4] Billions of decisions concerning health and safety are made each day in the United States. Only a minute proportion of these decisions is subject to a specific regulatory standard; and of this minute proportion, only a tiny fraction can be monitored by regulatory agencies. Most decisions are made by individual citizens concerning their own welfare: what and how much to eat, how to drive and cross streets, what products to buy and how to use them. The health and safety attributes ascribed to purchased goods and services result from engineering judgments, semi-informed guesses, and chance, as conditioned by regulation. Few of these processes are even conceptually subject to regulation by

2. Murray L. Weidenbaum and Robert DeFina, "The Cost of Federal Regulation of Economic Activity"; Arthur Anderson and Co., *Cost of Government Regulation Study for the Business Roundtable;* Roger G. Noll, *Reforming Regulation: An Evaluation of the Ash Council Proposals;* and other volumes in the series of Brookings Studies in the Regulation of Economic Activity.

3. Mitchell, "Silent Spring/Solid Majorities"; and Lave, "Health, Safety, and Environmental Regulations," pp. 135–37.

4. Larry E. Ruff, "Federal Environmental Regulation," app., pp. 251–346; Richard Zeckhauser and Albert Nichols, "The Occupational Safety and Health Administration: An Overview," pp. 163–248; and James Q. Wilson, ed., *The Politics of Regulation.*

federal government agencies. Like traffic laws, regulations are seldom regularly enforced.

Far from being able to do the whole job, regulatory agencies can do so little that they must be used carefully if they are to have any effect. Their first task must be to curtail the worst abuses, not wasting time on unimportant issues, and their second task must be to influence but make no pretense of controlling the decisions of manufacturers and consumers.[5] The latter depends on presenting these nongovernmental decisionmakers with facts, analyses, and a framework for making decisions and changing the perception of the importance of health and safety. For example, presenting an analysis of the facts might convince motorcyclists to wear helmets, while a decision framework might enable them to integrate the facts and analyses and help them think about their choices; perceptions can be changed by showing that motorcycle accidents are more costly to the rider and his family than had been supposed.

Setting priorities and influencing other decisionmakers is a radically different way of thinking about social regulation. It is a middle course between complete reliance on market regulation through caveat emptor and government control of design and production. The agencies have tended to act as if the latter were their mandate, as if their regulations alone had to accomplish socially desirable goals. They have received harsh criticism for failing to set and enforce regulations to prevent every unfortunate event from lung cancer deaths among asbestos workers to pollution episodes. Reacting to criticism that hundreds of carcinogenic and other toxic chemicals in the workplace are unregulated, the Occupational Safety and Health Administration has sought to regulate many more substances; yet redoubling its efforts has not succeeded in increasing the number of new regulations published each year. Similar examples can be given for each regulatory agency, since each finds that promulgating a new regulation requires thousands of professional man-hours and years of calendar time.

Regulatory Reform

Economists have long advocated that government decisions in general and regulatory decisions in particular can be improved by subjecting the

5. Michael S. Baram, *Alternatives to Regulation for Managing Risks to Health, Safety, and Environment.*

alternatives to benefit-cost analysis. But this method has aroused a range of reactions, as the following quotations demonstrate:

The limitations on the usefulness of benefit/cost analysis in the context of health, safety, and environmental regulatory decisionmaking are so severe that they militate against its use altogether.[6]

*   *   *

... [risk-benefit analysis is] the invention of those who do not wish to regulate, or to be regulated, and ... its primary use in governmental decision-making is to avoid taking action which is necessary or desirable in order to truly protect the health of the public or the integrity of the environment.[7]

*   *   *

Decision makers are chosen for their capacity to make judgments. The notion that product safety standards should be accepted or rejected on the basis of whether a quotient is less than or equal to unity overlooks this decision-making capacity. Cost-benefit analysis should be a part of, rather than a substitute for, the decision-making process.[8]

*   *   *

We do not really need a cost-benefit analysis to tell us that when the Interstate Commerce Commission restricts entry, it is going to have adverse effects on consumers. We do need cost-benefit analysis where the decision involves the kinds of uncertainties, consequences, and ramifications in the complex social environment that are entailed in many health and safety regulations—social regulators need all the help they can get in making these very difficult judgements....

We recommend: (1) Adoption of legislation which requires all agencies (both executive and independent) to perform cost-benefit analyses in all rule-making proceedings.[9]

An understanding of the regulatory muddle provides insights into the current formulation of proposals for regulatory reform.[10] Some agencies desire to shorten the process of setting standards and to curtail judicial review so that they can get on with their job. These modifications could

6. *Federal Regulation and Regulatory Reform,* Report by the Subcommittee on Oversight and Investigations of the House Committee on Interstate and Foreign Commerce, p. 515.

7. Burke K. Zimmerman, "Risk-Benefit Analysis: The Cop-Out of Governmental Regulation," p. 44.

8. Warren J. Prunella, "A Qualitative Assessment of Cost-Benefit Analysis and Its Application in the Area of Product Safety," p. 11.

9. *Cost-Benefit Analysis: Wonder Tool or Mirage?* Report together with Minority Views by the Subcommittee on Oversight and Investigations of the House Committee on Interstate and Foreign Commerce, Committee Print 96-IFC 62, 96 Cong. 2 sess. (Government Printing Office, 1980), pp. 42 and 48.

10. Christopher C. DeMuth, "Constraining Regulatory Costs," pt. 1: "The White House Review Programs," pp. 13–36; and DeMuth, "Constraining Regulatory Costs," pt. 2: "The Regulatory Budget," pp. 29–44.

serve to double or even triple the annual number of new regulations. Salient facts emerge during the current process, however, that result in better regulations. Furthermore, litigation is a formal process for resolving conflicts; if litigation is curtailed, the conflicts will not disappear but will only resurface in another guise.

A one-house veto or more extensive judicial review would serve to reduce the number of new regulations and to weed out those that were politically objectionable. Public desires for enhanced health and safety, however, would be less well satisfied than at present. Making the system less responsive to public desires creates a problem, not a solution.

The basic proposal examined in this book involves tailoring regulations to accomplish the twin objectives of curtailing the worst abuses and influencing the myriad decisions not specifically covered by any regulation. This can be done by giving more attention to the scientific foundation of regulatory issues and by using quantitative analyses to set priorities and to produce exemplary standards.

Social regulation can be improved by four steps. The first, mentioned above, is deciding what to regulate. A major focus of criticism has been regulations that have little to do with social goals—for example, the Occupational Safety and Health Administration's requirement that toilet seats have a split front. This is not a frivolous objection, since attention is being given to an issue of second-order importance while first-order issues languish. The second step is to present information, prepare analyses, and provide decision frameworks that clarify the implications of regulatory alternatives. For example, information can enable unions to bargain for safer workplaces and consumers to select safer products; analyses and information can be used to convince a jury that an employer, manufacturer, or polluter was the cause of damage and ought to pay compensation to the victim; decision frameworks can provide a mechanism for crystallizing goals and for achieving them more efficiently. The third step is to ensure that regulations are appropriate and not more stringent than necessary.[11] Society does not have surplus resources for unnecessary protection. In addition, it is important to send the correct signals concerning desired and acceptable solutions to influence other decisionmakers. The fourth step is to implement the regulations efficiently

11. Council on Wage and Price Stability, "Environmental Protection Agency's Proposed Revisions to the National Ambient Air Quality Standard for Photochemical Oxidants"; COWPS, "Proposed Standard for Exposure to Cotton Dust"; and James C. Miller III, "Exposure to Coke Oven Emissions Proposed Standard."

and quickly, without endless litigation or unnecessary social costs. While conflict is inevitable (and valuable) in setting social goals, a more systematic decision framework and more careful analysis can serve to eliminate many of the unnecessary disagreements and misunderstandings. By carefully setting out goals and methods, it may be possible to eliminate litigation on specific standards.

Carefully specifying goals and decision frameworks is the key to enhancing social regulation. No longer should regulations consist only of statements of broad social goals. Vague statements of intent from Congress must be replaced with precisely defined goals; vague statements of findings from the regulatory agency must be replaced with precise statements of the relevant facts and uncertainties that are based on analysis of the implications of relevant alternatives.

This approach should not be confused with a simplistic belief that science will answer each question without value conflicts or political judgments. Quantitative analysis is a valuable input to regulatory decisions, but it does not provide unambiguous answers in most cases. Though analysis cannot replace judgment, it can inform those who must make decisions.

This truism about the value of data and analysis is dismissed by regulatory agencies on the grounds that either the data base or the theoretical foundation is inadequate for confident estimates.[12] Lacking scientific evidence, the agencies are stuck with visceral estimates and political accommodations as the only bases for policy. This book demonstrates that quantitative analysis is possible and that it provides important information for regulatory decisions.

Altering regulation to focus on setting priorities and influencing other decisionmakers requires a substantial restructuring of current agencies. More comprehensive data collection and analysis has a number of costs, not only the direct cost of collection and analysis but also the associated cost of prolonging the initial states of the regulatory process. A substantial staff of professionals would be required for this work. More resources and time would have to be invested in the initial stages of each regulation, and this implies that fewer regulations could be issued by the agency.

12. Gio Batta Gori, "The Regulation of Carcinogenic Hazards," pp. 256–61; J. L. Radomski, "Evaluating the Role of Environmental Chemicals in Human Cancer," pp. 27–44; and memorandum, Arthur C. Upton, director of the National Cancer Institute, to the commissioner of the Food and Drug Administration, "Quantitative Risk Assessment."

This approach, however, could also lead to having more regulations in force, since there would be less ground for challenging each one and more deference from the courts as it became clear that the agencies were prepared to justify their regulations with scientific data and analysis. Perhaps the increase in scientific staff could be offset by a reduction in the requirement for lawyers to defend what currently appear to be arbitrary decisions. The additional data and analysis, however, could also provide new targets for litigation. The more carefully a regulatory agency clarifies the basis of its regulations and presents facts showing adherence to legislative goals, the more likely the resulting regulation is to be challenged in the political rather than the legal arena, if it is challenged at all.

The potential contribution of this analytic approach is expressed in the answers to a series of questions that occur throughout this study:

—Are there simple procedures for setting priorities within an agency?

—Can a set of decision frameworks be specified that define priorities, provide sensible regulations, and help both agency and other decision-makers?

—What data and analysis are required for this approach? Are required data available and relatively inexpensive to gather and could the analysis be done by government employees on a routine basis?

—To what extent have these techniques been applied already in regulatory decisionmaking and how helpful have they been?

—Can the analysis be applied to the range of regulatory activity, including such emotion-laden areas as health?

—Do the techniques offer a contribution commensurate with the manpower, time, and general difficulty required?

Chapter 2 describes six decision frameworks currently in use and two proposed frameworks, showing how they could be used to set priorities and make decisions. Chapter 3 clarifies the necessary scientific background and nature of the assumptions necessary to apply each framework. Chapter 4 applies these eight decision frameworks to food additives and contaminants, sketching the nature of the decision that would result from each framework. Although food additives is perhaps the most difficult area to attempt quantitative analysis, there remains the question of whether all these frameworks can be applied to other health and safety decisions. A more general review is undertaken in chapter 5, with applications of the eight decision frameworks to a number of cases. Chapter 6 is an attempt to draw together the implications of this investigation and to clarify how social regulation can be enhanced.

CHAPTER TWO

Eight Frameworks for Regulation

THE FRAMEWORKS used to guide analysis and the decisions made regarding proposed health and safety regulations are inextricably linked. For example, if an agency is required by law to ban any substance shown to be a carcinogen, little or nothing is gained by an elaborate analysis of the economic and other implications of alternative decisions. The decision framework establishes priorities among issues and changes the way both regulators and nongovernmental decisionmakers view health and safety issues. Choosing a decision framework and using it consistently is perhaps the most important device for influencing the billions of decisions governing health and safety that are outside the control of federal regulators. Failure to appreciate the importance of the decision framework is the root of much of the criticism of social regulation. Legislation such as the Toxic Substances Control Act; the Federal Insecticide, Fungicide, and Rodenticide Act; and the Consumer Product Safety Act requires analysis of benefits, costs, and risks in formulating a regulation.[1] Unfortunately subject areas such as carcinogenicity lack a firm scientific foundation for an analysis of this kind, and agencies often lack resources to carry out analysis for those areas having a scientific foundation. Legislation such as the Delaney Clause is highly specific in requiring a ban,[2] but occasionally

1. Michael S. Baram, "Regulation of Health, Safety and Environmental Quality and the Use of Cost-Benefit Analysis," pp. 46, 59–60, 75–76; and L. E. Erickson, "Issues and Experiences in Applying Benefit Cost Analysis to Health and Safety Standards," app. A and E.
2. The so-called Delaney Clause resulted from hearings held by Congressman James Delaney of New York and is found in the Food Additives Amendment of 1958 to the Food, Drug, and Cosmetic Act of 1938 (72 Stat. 1786). It states in part that "no additive shall be deemed to be safe if it is found . . . to induce cancer in man or animal."

8

this action is so counter to public desires that the agency is condemned for carrying out the legislation, for example, for banning saccharin.

Decision Frameworks

Six frameworks for making regulatory decisions are currently being used and two have been proposed. The frameworks range, roughly, from those requiring the least theory, data, and analysis and offering the least flexibility to those at the opposite pole; they include market regulation, no-risk, technology-based standards, risk-risk (proposed), risk-benefit, cost-effectiveness, regulatory budget (proposed), and benefit-cost.[3]

Market Regulation

Economic theory has formalized the 200-year-old insight of Adam Smith that competitive markets are efficient. In particular (under a set of stringent assumptions including complete information, no transaction costs, rational consumers and producers, no economies of scale in production, and no externalities), a competitive market produces an efficient (or Pareto optimal) equilibrium in the sense that no one can be made better off without making at least one person worse off.[4] This efficiency principle also holds for situations involving risk, such as hazardous products or jobs, although still more stringent assumptions are needed.[5]

Each person in such an economy presumably would decide what is best for him by looking at the array of available products and jobs. Since risk is an undesirable attribute, all risky products and jobs having no compensating attributes would be eliminated, and individuals would scrutinize those risky products and jobs that offered higher pay or some other

---

3. Arranging the frameworks is not so simple. For example, risk-benefit analysis requires as much information as benefit-cost analysis, although it is less formal. While more than a single dimension is involved, the ordering is roughly accurate. See the bibliography for additional references.

4. Gerard Debreu, *Theory of Value: An Axiomatic Analysis of Economic Equilibrium;* and Kenneth J. Arrow and F. H. Hahn, *General Competitive Analysis.*

5. Kenneth J. Arrow, "Limited Knowledge and Economic Analysis," pp. 1–10; and Jacques H. Dreze, ed., *Allocation under Uncertainty: Equilibrium and Optimality.*

advantage to determine which should be taken. Under the restrictive assumptions, government regulation would be unnecessary.

Clearly the U.S. economy does not satisfy the host of restrictive assumptions; both buyers and sellers can often influence price, many effects are transmitted outside the marketplace, and often buyers and sellers are woefully ignorant of the health and safety implications of a product. Market equilibrium is inefficient and a case can be made for government intervention. Some economists caution Americans to eschew perfection, arguing that they would be better off in the long run by tolerating these relatively minor evils instead of erecting a huge, self-defeating regulatory structure. Regulation requires resources, but more important, it is virtually impossible to regulate so that incentives are not distorted, and this often leads to even greater inefficiency than in the unregulated market— for example, transportation regulation, particularly of airlines and trains.[6] Many economists argue that regulation is justified only when serious violations of the assumptions occur, and then only if the regulation can be relatively efficient.[7]

An outstanding controversy concerns whether the current U.S. economy is essentially competitive and the consumers well informed. One side claims that the economy has hardly a hint of competition and that most consumers and workers are ignorant.[8] The other side sees intense competition, even within such oligopolistic industries as automobiles and airlines.[9] Each side can muster persuasive examples, although general proof is impossible. Society has tended to sway with the winds of intellectual discourse, with gusts of regulation and then deregulation, as in transportation, for example. There is general agreement, however, that the economy is basically governed by the free market and that some regulation is necessary. Successful regulators are pragmatic. Doctrinaire positions concerning government control or laissez-faire are interpreted within the context of each case, with the ultimate outcome dependent on the nature of price control, consumer and worker ignorance, and magnitude of risk.

6. Theodore E. Keeler, "Domestic Trunk Airline Deregulation: An Economic Evaluation," pp. 75–149; and Paul W. MacAvoy and John W. Snow, eds., *Railroad Revitalization and Regulatory Reform,* p. 6.

7. George J. Stigler, *The Citizen and the State: Essays on Regulation;* and Milton Friedman, *Capitalism and Freedom.*

8. John Kenneth Galbraith, *Economics and the Public Purpose;* Galbraith, *The New Industrial State;* and Robert L. Heilbroner, *The Limits of American Capitalism,* pp. 1–61.

9. Friedman, *Capitalism and Freedom;* and Stigler, *The Citizen and the State.*

Whether to license auto mechanics or to regulate sodium nitrite is decided by consideration of the specific facts and risks rather than by the doctrinaire view that government should or should not regulate risky situations.

In summary, the decision to use the market to regulate risk puts faith in consumer information and judgments. It sees the costs of bureaucracy constraining private decisions as larger than costs arising from market imperfections and advises accepting current imperfections rather than creating a regulatory morass.

No-Risk

The philosophy behind the Delaney Clause of the Food, Drug, and Cosmetic Act, and food additive amendments generally, is that the public should be exposed to no additional or unnecessary risk. Carcinogens cannot be added to foods or remain as residuals in meat since this might increase the risk of cancer; according to the Clean Air Act Amendments of 1970, air pollution levels must be sufficiently low to protect the population from adverse effects, presumably even the most sensitive members.

This approach has great appeal as rhetoric. To argue that carcinogens ought to be permitted in the food supply is to argue that society must allow higher than necessary risks of cancer. Why should any unnecessary exposure be tolerated, even if the risk appears to be small?

The no-risk framework has the advantage of requiring little data and analysis and precludes agonizing about the decision to be made. According to the Delaney Clause, the only question is whether a food additive has been shown to be a carcinogen in humans or animals. Thus data (on the quality, variety, and price of food) concerning the consequences of banning may not be considered. The Delaney Clause has a simple, straightforward answer to a complicated question: ban a substance if there is evidence of carcinogenicity. Frameworks other than market regulation require answers to a set of complicated questions: What level of risks are acceptable? What benefits would serve to offset the risks? Can animal bioassays be relied on to demonstrate human carcinogenicity?[10]

10. Interagency Regulatory Liaison Group, "Scientific Bases for Identifying Potential Carcinogens and Estimating Their Risks," pp. 22–61; National Academy of Sciences, *Food Safety Policy: Scientific and Societal Considerations*, pp. 5-21 through 5-25; and "Identification, Classification and Regulation of Toxic Substances Posing a Potential Occupational Carcinogenic Risk," *Federal Register*, vol. 42 (October 4, 1977), pp. 54156–67.

Can the potency of a substance for humans be demonstrated under current exposure levels? If one requires simple answers to these questions or distrusts the complicated answers given by experts, no-risk offers an appealing solution.

Unfortunately the answers are too simple. Virtually all "natural" foods contain trace elements of carcinogens, including biological contaminants and pesticides. The Food and Drug Administration treats natural foods differently than food additives; apparently it is less troublesome to die from a cancer induced by a natural food than from one induced by a food additive. Does anyone seriously propose to ban all foods with trace levels of carcinogens? Does it make sense to treat those with trace amounts in the same way as those with large amounts of potent carcinogens?

In practice the Food and Drug Administration considers, at least indirectly, the potency of each substance and the effects on the food supply.[11] As shown in chapter 4, the agency agonizes over decisions concerning carcinogens when banning would reduce the food supply or merely deprive Americans of some cherished food. Any attempt to impose consistency runs into the impossibility of eliminating risks generally and carcinogens particularly. It is less obvious, however, that they could not be eliminated from a narrow class of substances such as food additives.

If society were concerned solely or even principally with the safety of food, the no-risk approach would be an appropriate guide for regulation, but society is concerned with many other issues as well. People eat foods they know to be harmful to their health and they indulge in a range of habits indicating that health is neither their sole objective nor even a very important one.[12] For example, in addition to overeating and not eating wholesome foods in a balanced diet, people smoke cigarettes, live in cities with polluted air, and work in occupations they know pose risks of accidents and chronic disease.[13] Attempting to legislate safety by banning food additives that lower cost, enhance flavor and appearance, or increase

11. Richard A. Merrill, "Regulating Carcinogens in Food: A Legislator's Guide to the Food Safety Provisions of the Federal Food, Drug, and Cosmetic Act," pp. 245–46; Peter Barton Hutt, "Food Regulation," pp. 521–24, and 553; and Richard A. Merrill, "Federal Regulation of Cancer-Causing Chemicals," chap. 2: "FDA Regulation of Environmental Contaminants," pp. 21–25.

12. NAS, *Food Safety Policy;* Victor R. Fuchs, "Some Economic Aspects of Mortality in Developed Countries"; and Fuchs, "Economics, Health, and Post Industrial Society," pp. 153–82.

13. Lester B. Lave and others, "Economic Impact of Preventive Medicine," pp. 675–705; Lester B. Lave and Eugene P. Seskin, *Air Pollution and Human Health,* chap. 10; and Robert S. Smith, "Compensating Wage Differentials and Public Policy: A Review."

convenience is like attempting to legislate morality: the rhetorical appeal is evident, but regulation can hope to affect only a tiny proportion of the relevant risk, and at rapidly increasing cost.

The three principal objections to this framework are the current misallocation of resources, the closing of the door to future solutions, and the inconsistency in government policy. In addition this framework cannot distinguish between a toxin that is extremely weak and to which few people are exposed and a potent carcinogen to which nearly the entire population is exposed. Insofar as there are many carcinogens and it is costly to ban at least some of them, this framework does not help to develop priorities—which substance should be treated first?—or guidelines—what level of safety ought to be sought where banning is infeasible? Instead, it sends regulators scurrying off to devote much of their attention to relatively benign substances by giving all toxins equal priority.[14] Thus the framework is a pernicious guide to regulators confronted with complicated problems.

Although Congress has written the no-risk framework into legislation, it is a straw man unworthy of serious consideration. Even the attempt to maintain the facade is increasingly recognized by the regulatory agencies to be impossible. For example, the Food and Drug Administration has attempted to define a "negligible" risk level; any risk below a level of one in one million lifetimes would be considered to be zero for regulatory purposes.[15] The Environmental Protection Agency has taken an even more hostile view of the no-risk framework:

A requirement that the risk from atmospheric carcinogen emissions be reduced to zero would produce massive social dislocations, given the pervasiveness of at least minimal levels of carcinogenic emissions in key American industries. Since few such industries would soon operate in compliance with zero-emission standards, closure would be the only legal alternative. Among the important activities affected would be the generation of electricity from either coal-burning or nuclear energy; the manufacturing of steel; the mining, smelting, or refining of virtually any mineral (e.g., copper, iron, lead, zinc, and limestone); the manufacture of synthetic organic chemicals; and the refining, storage, or dispensing of any petroleum product. That Congress had no clear intention of mandating such results seems self-evident.[16]

14. Paul F. Deisler, Jr., "Dealing with Industrial Health Risks," p. 8.
15. "Chemical Compounds in Food-Producing Animals," *Federal Register,* vol. 42 (February 22, 1977), p. 10421.
16. "National Emission Standards for Identifying, Assessing and Regulating Airborne Substances Posing a Risk of Cancer," *Federal Register,* vol. 42 (October 10, 1979), p. 58660.

Technology-Based Standards

Recognizing the difficulty of attempting to estimate the health and safety effects of a proposed standard (much less the problem of quantifying these effects), a number of agencies have placed their reliance on engineering judgments.[17] The best available control technology has been required extensively by the Environmental Protection Agency in regulating air and water pollution. This framework has the simplicity of requiring the estimation of neither benefits nor costs. The data and analysis required are for identifying a hazard and then for making the engineering judgment as to the best available control technology. This framework requires a second set of information for determining the best available control technology in addition to the carcinogenicity data required for the no-risk framework.

In practice, however, there is never a best technology but only successively more expensive and stringent technologies. For example, the effectiveness of an electrostatic precipitator in removing suspended particles from air is proportional to the collector plate area; effectiveness can be increased by increasing the area. In practice, engineering judgment defines best available control technology as a finite collector plate area, even though further increases in plate area would improve (minutely) the effectiveness of collection. At some point additional abatement is unwarranted because social costs exceed social benefits; but even then technology is available that would abate emissions further. In practice, best available control technology embodies implicit assumptions about the benefits and costs of further abatement.

The crucial issue in implementing this framework at present is the financial burden each industry can bear. As long as an industry is not in danger of bankruptcy, a technology that lowered emissions would be considered acceptable. Sufficient uncertainty exists about what cost level would endanger an industry that regulators rarely impose standards that come close to doing so.

In summary, the primary advantage of technology-based standards is that they require no formal evidence on costs or benefits; the only data required are those necessary for good engineering judgments. The resulting standard, however, will depend on regulators' perceptions of industry profitability. If an area is populated by an industry teetering on the brink

17. Larry E. Ruff, "Federal Environmental Regulation," pp. 279–82, 299–303.

of bankruptcy, best available control technology will be weak and few emissions will be abated. If the industry is profitable, it will require large expenditures. There is more than a theoretical possibility that the first regulation in an industry would press it to the limit of its ability to afford regulation, leaving no financial resources to handle later regulations that might be far more important. Rather than being a framework for lowering risk or even for using engineering judgments, technology-based standards is a framework for regulating economic activity through imposing costs arbitrarily among industries until all are at the same minimal level of profit.

Risk-Risk: Direct

Even if maximum protection were desired, the Delaney Clause would be a poor framework because it requires banning carcinogens. Some toxic substances, such as food additives and fungicides, prevent contamination of food, and thus it is desirable to weigh one risk against the other, as recognized by the Food and Drug Administration and the Department of Agriculture in the proposed risk-risk analysis.[18] Balancing the toxicity of a substance against the enhanced protection it brings can be done from either of two perspectives. The narrow perspective is that of balancing the risk to the consumer of the additive against the direct health benefits. Sodium nitrite may be a carcinogen, but it protects against botulism; the risk of cancer must be balanced against that of botulism. The broad perspective takes account of both producers and consumers as shown below.

Since the risk-risk framework allows beneficial health effects to be considered along with adverse health effects, it is more flexible than no-risk. It and the remaining frameworks are qualitatively different from no-risk in that they require quantification of risk and at least partial estimation of benefits. If quantification were impossible, this framework could not be implemented because there would be no method for balancing unmatched risks (for example, chronic respiratory disease versus broken legs). Quantification is particularly difficult for the effects of toxic substances; thus this and the remaining frameworks are subject to the caution of those who contend that potency cannot be estimated from animal bioassays, or at least that potency for humans at low doses cannot be

18. U.S. Food and Drug Administration and the U.S. Department of Agriculture, "FDA's and USDA's Action Regarding Nitrite."

inferred reliably.[19] The ability to estimate human risks will be treated in chapter 3.

All frameworks except the first two allow the possibility of labeling or other action short of banning.[20] This gives wider choice to individuals, permitting them different life-styles. Insofar as choice and diversity are important, alternatives to banning are important.

While the risk-risk framework provides somewhat greater flexibility, it still precludes consideration of nonhealth effects. Conceptually it is a small step since it merely includes both the health risks and health benefits of a proposal. In practice it appears to be a major improvement over the no-risk framework—where it is applicable. Cases such as sodium nitrite where the risk-risk framework is invaluable, are the exception. Few substances offer a direct health benefit to the consumer other than drugs, products for which the Food and Drug Administration already uses this framework. The framework is of limited interest because it is of such limited applicability.

Risk-Risk: Indirect

The advantage of the risk-risk framework over the no-risk framework is that it permits wider analysis of risks. One way of stating the objective is that society desires to minimize the adverse health effects associated with a given food such as bacon. Thus society would permit nitrite in bacon if the improvement in the health of consumers from botulism protection exceeded the decrement in health from the risk of cancer. Yet it is evident that the direct risk-risk framework takes only the first step of considering the health of the person consuming the food. People are also associated with the production and distribution of food; society desires to minimize the adverse health effects associated with producing as well as consuming bacon (for a fixed level of production). Workers would not

19. Gio Batta Gori, "The Regulation of Carcinogenic Hazards," pp. 256–61; J. L. Radomski, "Evaluating the Role of Environmental Chemicals in Human Cancer," pp. 27–44; memorandum, Arthur C. Upton, director of the National Cancer Institute, to the commissioner of the Food and Drug Administration, "Quantitative Risk Assessment"; and National Academy of Sciences, *Saccharin: Technical Assessment of Risks and Benefits,* p. ES-5.

20. See NAS, *Food Safety Policy,* pp. 4–17, 8–5; and Oliver E. Williamson, "Public Policy on Saccharin: The Decision Process Approach and Its Alternatives," in Robert Crandall and Lester B. Lave, eds., *The Scientific Basis of Health, Safety, and Environmental Regulation.*

countenance a regulation that offered consumers a small amount of protection at the cost of a large increase in risk to workers.

Since every human activity is risky, a regulation that requires more man-hours to produce a unit of food would increase the exposure and presumably the occupational risk of workers. The indirect risk-risk framework includes occupational risks associated with each additive or contaminant (see the appendix for some methods that might be used to estimate these occupational risks).

One qualification to this approach is that consumers often are unaware of food risks, while workers are likely to have better information and receive a wage premium to take occupational risks. Furthermore, there is some selectivity of workers for a particular job, at least limited flexibility to change jobs or even to quit if the risks are too high, and some ability to remain alert when risks are highest.[21]

The indirect risk-risk framework is an important generalization since it allows consideration of implied health risks to workers. The difficulty is estimating health risks. As a first step in the analysis, assume that the same quantity of a regulated product would be produced as had been produced before. The immediate effect on workers might be estimated by assuming that the average rates of accidents and occupational disease in an industry would apply to the additional effort required by the proposed regulation, for example, additional feed grains to fatten steers because diethylstilbestrol is banned in particular, if banning it required a 10 percent increase in corn production, accidents and occupational disease among corn farmers would be estimated to increase by 10 percent. There are a series of ripple effects, however. The additional farming will require more seed, fertilizer, machinery, and fuel; these in turn will require more steel, coal, and so forth, each of which will involve occupational accidents and disease. Some preliminary notions for quantifying such ripple effects are discussed in the appendix.

Risk-Benefit

Unlike the risk-benefit framework, the three previous ones do not allow consideration of nonhealth effects. The folly of refusing to consider these effects is illustrated by examining one's own choices. For example, most people are willing to risk the minute chance of biological contamina-

21. Smith, "Compensating Wage Differentials and Public Policy."

tion rather than to be bothered with boiling drinking water. They are willing to undertake additional risks in order to get rewards such as additional income and recreational stimulation. For example, there is a risk premium in the pay of workers in hazardous occupations to attract them in the face of the higher risks.[22] These premiums can be extremely high, as for test pilots, steeplejacks, and divers working deep in the ocean. If the effect of a regulation is to lower risk minutely at the cost of a vast increase in price, a lessening of choice or convenience, harm to the environment, or a sacrifice in social goals generally, society should not be satisfied. The frameworks previously mentioned suffer from their lack of recognition of other social goals such as the ecosystem, endangered species, and individual freedoms.[23]

Under the risk-benefit framework, regulators would be enjoined to balance the general benefits of a proposed regulation against its general risks. This framework is intended to be somewhat vague, with all effects being enumerated, but with full quantification and valuation being left to the general wisdom of the regulators. The framework may account for cost, convenience, and even preferences in an attempt to balance benefits against risks.[24] A vast array of frameworks can come under the risk-benefit heading, from balancing health risks against health benefits (like the risk-risk indirect framework) to consideration of all risks, costs, and benefits. The framework has an immediate appeal to congressmen and regulators since it is a general instruction to consider all social factors in arriving at a decision. While no one can oppose considering all relevant factors, no one has specified precisely how this is to be done.

The intellectual difficulty with this framework is its lack of precise definition. Are only health risks to be considered, or are risks to the present and future environment (air, water, louseworts, snail darters, and

22. Ibid.; and Richard Thaler and Sherwin Rosen, "The Value of Saving a Life: Evidence from the Labor Market," pp. 265–98. The various studies attempt to control for other factors affecting pay, such as years of training.

23. Lester B. Lave and Lester Silverman, "Economic Costs of Energy-Related Environmental Pollution," pp. 619–23.

24. Chauncey Starr, "Benefit-Cost Studies in Sociotechnical Systems"; Starr, "Social Benefit Versus Technological Risk"; NAS, *Product Safety;* Cyril Comar, "SO$_2$ Regulations"; Richard Wilson, "Direct Testimony in the Matter of Proposed Regulations . . . for Toxic Substances Posing a Potential Occupational Carcinogenic Risk"; Bernard L. Cohen, "Society Valuation of Life Saving in Radiation Protection and Other Contents"; Thomas H. Jukes, "Diethylstilbestrol in Beef Production: What Is the Risk?" and Richard C. Schwing, "Expenditures to Reduce Mortality Risk and Increase Longevity."

EIGHT FRAMEWORKS FOR REGULATION

tundra) relevant? If they are not, the framework is no more complete than the previous one, and if they are, how can the risks to louseworts be added to those to the health of our great grandchildren and of current workers? Similarly, there is no guidance about how to quantify benefits: what is the value of an increase in the supply of food or electricity?

This is the most general and flexible framework, but one despairs at its implementation. Is it more than an injunction that decisionmakers ought to think broadly about the risks and benefits of their decisions? Insofar as decisionmakers are suspicious of quantification or do not believe that it can be done with confidence, this framework serves to broaden their consideration, but it still relies on their intuitive judgments. While it is desirable to broaden the scope of matters to be considered, the failure to define what is irrelevant has lengthened hearings and complicated the record. The risk-benefit framework makes no pretense at being an automatic decisionmaking tool. It forces regulators to consider a broad set of costs and outcomes; they cannot abdicate their responsibility by examining only a narrow set of effects or appealing to some arbitrary criterion as they can under the no-risk framework. The risk-benefit framework, however, has produced decisions and justifications that seem arbitrary and inexplicable; it has been a step forward, but it is too unsatisfactory to be more than a transitional step.

Cost-Effectiveness

Many organizations, private and public, find themselves attempting to increase output even though their current budget is fixed. The intellectual contributions in defining this problem and developing rules to solve it have come from the Department of Defense. Although cost-effectiveness is often thought erroneously to refer to getting some specific project done at lowest cost, the concept is much broader, referring to accomplishing some general objective at lowest cost. President Eisenhower's secretary of defense, Charles Wilson, described the goal succinctly as an attempt to "get the most bang for the buck."

How can a goal be achieved within a fixed budget? For example, the goal of the National Cancer Institute is to lower the cancer death rate. It might achieve this goal by devoting resources to basic research, clinical trials testing new treatment techniques, public education, prevention by lowering the amounts of carcinogens in the environment, early detection of cancer, or the provision of more treatment. How should the fixed budget be allocated among these competing programs to lower both the incidence of cancer and the occurrence of death and lesser effects?

Mathematically, this is a problem of maximization under constraints; the solution is to equate the effectiveness of the last dollar spent on each activity. For this example, the National Cancer Institute ought to allocate funds among the programs (taking care that the most effective projects are done first within each program) by testing the effectiveness of each dollar. The first increment of funds should be given to the program where it would be estimated to save the most lives. The second increment of funds should be allocated by the same criterion, perhaps going to the same program. As each successive increment of funds is allocated, the number of lives it saves should fall (since the best projects were done first). When all funds have been allocated, it should be true that the last increment of funds to each program would be expected to save approximately the same number of lives. If not, then funds should be reallocated by recalling them from the program where they are least effective and giving them to the program where they are most effective. Mathematically, the ratio of lives saved to dollars expended (for the last increment of funds) should be equal across programs when all funds have been allocated. As long as the ratios are not equal, additional lives could be saved for the same budget by removing funds from the program with the lowest ratio and adding them to the program with the highest ratio.

This criterion of the effectiveness of incremental or marginal dollars is often mistaken for the effectiveness of total dollars. The confused objective is to equate across programs the ratio of lives saved per dollar expended with the total expenditures. This criterion is not efficient since funds could be reallocated so as to save more lives for the same budget.

If the goal is properly stated and if the budget is appropriate, cost-effectiveness analysis will lead to the same decisions as the more elaborate frameworks; this is not true for no-risk, technology-based standards, and risk-risk. Thus it would be equivalent to the more elaborate frameworks under the proper assumptions, or it could be a parody of them if the goal or budget is incorrect.

Cost-effectiveness offers a major advantage over benefit-cost analysis in that it does not require an explicit value for the social cost of premature death (or other untraded goods). Assumptions about these values are built into the goal and budget (for example, maximize lives saved for a fixed budget) but need not be stated explicitly. The flip side of this advantage, however, is that errors in stating the goal or in determining the budget can lead to bad decisions, and there is no internal mechanism for showing the errors in these decisions and the changes in goals or budget that are necessary.

Regulatory Budget

Cost-effectiveness is a good framework if the relevant costs are being measured in the analysis. Unfortunately when the only costs considered are those of the regulatory agency, the framework will misallocate resources because only one subset of the total costs of the regulation to the entire economy is being considered. The agencies have little or no reason to consider the costs that their regulations impose on others unless the costs are so high that industry bankruptcy is a relevant possibility. The agencies are instructed to protect the environment, consumers, or workers without any apparent limits on their ability to impose costs on others. That the resulting regulations are not universally perceived as desirable can be judged from the comments of the affected companies and the fact that the federal government has often exempted itself from the regulations or has been slow in implementing them.

An idea originating in the Council of Economic Advisers under Charles Schultze was to give each regulatory agency an implementation budget in the form of a limit on the total annual costs that its regulations could impose.[25] For example, the Environmental Protection Agency might be given an implementation budget of $10 billion a year, which would mean that the costs of implementing its air, water, solid waste, radiation, and pesticide regulations could not exceed $10 billion in that year. Each agency would develop an implementation budget request, just as it currently develops its operating budget request. The administration would coordinate and impose priorities on the agencies, and then Congress would react to these requests, modifying them as necessary.

The regulatory budget is one method of implementing cost-effectiveness analysis. The goals needed for the framework are stated in the legislation for each agency, supplemented by whatever informal instructions

25. Personal communication with Charles L. Schultze. See U.S. Department of Commerce, *Regulatory Reform Seminar: Proceedings and Background Paper*, pp. 17–31; Christopher C. DeMuth, "Constraining Regulatory Costs," pt. 1: "The White House Review Programs," pp. 13–36; DeMuth, "Constraining Regulatory Costs," pt. 2: "The Regulatory Budget," pp. 29–44; and William Nordhaus and Robert Litan, "A Regulatory Budget for the United States."

arise from hearings, appropriations, Office of Management and Budget directives, or presidential intervention. The internal and implementation budgets would be considered and approved by Congress, based on each agency's data on effectiveness. A major advantage of the framework is that it would elicit from the agencies a clearer indication of their priorities and would enable Congress to make more intelligent decisions regarding social values.

The principal difficulties with the framework are in estimating the costs and effects of each regulation. Where a control device must be added to a smokestack, there is debate about the cost of the device and about its expected lifetime, maintenance, and reliability. For a new piece of technology, these difficulties might perhaps introduce a factor-of-two difference in estimated costs. When the regulation will require a change in process or result in banning a substance, the costs become much more uncertain. If there is a factor-of-five-or-ten difference between reasonable high and low estimates of implementation costs, the regulatory budget cannot provide a helpful constraint.

Discipline might be exerted by the use of ex post reviews of previous cost estimates and the resulting experience. Even for regulations that have been implemented, however, it is difficult to estimate the additional costs due to the regulation. In addition, several years would elapse before sufficient experience accumulated to estimate costs retrospectively; disciplining the agency for bad cost estimates during a previous administration would make little sense.

Excluding uncertain or indirect costs (while estimating only direct costs or those that can be confidently quantified) would give a terrible set of incentives to the regulatory agency. For example, banning a substance would minimize direct costs, even though it might impose very substantial indirect costs. Similarly, counting only current costs would lead the agency to design a regulation to impose costs in the future.

Estimating the accomplishments or benefits of a regulation is even more difficult, but this problem is common to all the frameworks from risk-risk to benefit-cost analysis. Good estimates of costs are required for the frameworks encompassed by cost-effectiveness and benefit-cost. There is no easy way to improve the quality of the cost and effectiveness estimates. They will necessarily be uncertain, and agencies will choose estimates from the end of the range that can be justified. This framework cannot be seen as a mechanical way of laying to rest the difficult questions of setting regulations, but it might serve to present more complete information in a useful framework to the correct decisionmakers.

A good deal of work remains to be done in exploring this framework. Seemingly subtle issues affect the outcome of the analysis. For example, the budget constraint can be stated for all regulatory agencies, for each division or program, or for "discretionary" funds. If trade-offs are made only within narrow programs, the overall result is unlikely to be satisfactory. For example, should the Food and Drug Administration be making trade-offs among food additives or among all activities under its purview that could enhance health? If the Food and Drug Administration were permitted to allocate time and funds among all activities, it might focus on cigarette smoking and ignore food additives. Some groups feel strongly about food additives and would protest a lack of regulatory attention to this area, even if the resources saved more lives by decreasing cigarette consumption.

How would the regulatory budget be determined? Agencies would request large budgets and be opposed by those who must pay implementation costs. The major advantage of this framework is precisely that it puts these issues of social values and of agency efficiency into a forum that facilitates their discussion and resolution and forces Congress to make these judgments. The resulting hearings will raise many relevant issues.

Academicians see the advantages of coherent, well thought out intellectual frameworks. For example, there is a misallocation of resources if some agency assumes, implicitly or explicitly, that the cost to society of premature death is greater than that assumed by another agency. Congressmen express shock at the notion that such a value exists. The political process presents an incremental approach, where a set of social values emerges from dozens of laws and decisions, much like the development of common law. Decisionmakers feel more confident in answering these questions for particular cases than in giving abstract uniform answers. While the regulatory budget is admirably matched to current American political institutions, the result is unlikely to be an intellectually coherent framework.

Benefit-Cost

This framework is similar to the general balancing of risks against benefits; the principal difference is that it is more quantitative and formal.

In addition to enumerating the various benefits of the regulation and then subjectively balancing benefits against costs, this framework would require quantification of the extent to which the benefits and costs vary with the level of regulation, and then would require each of these effects to be translated into dollars.

There are many controversial aspects to its application, including putting an explicit value on prolonging a life, quantifying other benefits, deciding the rate at which effects in the future are discounted to make them equivalent to current effects, and redistributing income.[26] Valuing benefits, or even deciding what is a benefit, runs into the diversity of cultural backgrounds, personal goals, fears, and time horizons. These difficulties are explored in chapters 4 and 5. Benefit-cost analysis is the most general and quantitative of the frameworks, and thus elicits the most information and requires the most analysis.[27]

Benefit-cost analysis is a sufficiently broad framework to be adapted to consider virtually any aspect of a regulation or public decision. The implications for those who gain or lose can be folded into the analysis. None of the objections to the framework have the effect of showing an inherent bias or blind spot in the analysis.

In practice, however, the picture is quite different. Benefit-cost analysis is often viewed, correctly, as a tool for defending the status quo. It is rarely used to consider who benefits or pays, and it focuses on the present, giving short shrift to even the near-term future with no importance for events more than a few decades in the future. Adjustment costs are often estimated to be higher than would be observed, reflecting a prejudice that the current situation must be the best one (when adjustment costs are not considered, the analysis is biased toward change). Finally, a number of simplifying assumptions are made that bias the analysis against change.

In a world where data are costly to gather and analyze and are rarely

26. National Academy of Sciences, *Analytical Studies for the U.S. Environmental Protection Agency,* vol. 2: *Decision Making in the Environmental Protection Agency,* app. D; Baruch Fischoff and others, "Approaches to Acceptable Risk," pp. 169–204; and Baram, "Regulation of Health, Safety, and Environmental Quality."

27. Benefit-cost analysis usually assumes fixed prices, wages, and discount rates. If the scope of project or projects being analyzed is sufficiently large, however, prices and discount rate must be determined within the analysis. Thus applying benefit-cost analysis to all health and safety decisions made by the Food and Drug Administration would require a determination of the appropriate discount rate and would probably specify more projects than the agency could afford to do immediately. In this sense the regulatory budget framework is a specialization of benefit-cost analysis.

conclusive, one must be content with uncertainty and with making educated guesses. The most important material should be considered first, leaving data and issues of lesser importance for future analysis, if warranted. This framework is especially good at interpreting economic data; economic issues have tended to be of first-order importance and thus the framework has raised the significant issues. The more important non-economic concerns are and the more remote the relationship to economic variables is, the less helpful this framework will be.

For example, when benefit-cost analysis is used within a profit-making corporation to enlighten an investment decision, economic issues are of central concern. In considering government investments in inland waterways, economic considerations are predominant, although a host of other issues must be considered. In considering whether the United States should purchase oil from a particular nation in the Middle East, economic considerations are dominated by political and more general ethical considerations. In moving from a corporate decision concerning an investment to purchasing oil from a particular nation, the relative importance of economic issues declines. The benefit-cost framework ceases to be comprehensive and loses any claim to being the sole factor in making the decision. Instead, it becomes a framework for raising issues, organizing information, and deriving quantification where possible.

Benefit-cost analysis is not the best framework for examining distributional questions since it offers no way of quantifying the desirability of transferring income from one individual to another. While it might be decided that a project has a beneficial redistribution of income, the net benefit cannot be quantified. Some ethicists (for example, the utilitarians) were able to deal with this issue theoretically by defining an optimal distribution of income; in practice these questions are hotly debated and decisions are specific to situations. None of the frameworks can be expected to handle this set of questions well.

A Comparison of Frameworks

The eight frameworks stretch from simple solutions (let the market do it or accept no unnecessary risk) to elaborate ones (identify all effects and value them in dollars). The range of problems is even greater, stretching from purely scientific ones (is nitrite a carcinogen?) to purely value conflicts (since so few people buckle their belts, should passive seat belts be required, even though they are more expensive and less effective than current belts?). Only by appreciating the complexity of problems and frameworks can there be an intelligent analysis of how to improve standard settings.

The issues of simplicity and the amount of data collection and analysis required are illustrated by proceeding from the no-risk to the benefit-cost framework. Flexibility in finding solutions and a broader purview of the issues are being purchased at the cost of collecting and analyzing more data and grappling with myriad problems, some of which have no solution. For example, how does society value a cancer today as against one occurring in twenty years? As against one occurring in 300 years? How is a risk of death of one in one million to be weighed against the risk of a broken leg of one in ten?

Four criteria might be used to compare frameworks:

The first is comprehensiveness. Are all the relevant issues encompassed within the framework? No-risk considers only carcinogenesis (or other health attributes); risk-risk considers all health consequences either to the consumer (direct) or more generally (indirect). Cost-effectiveness and the regulatory budget require examination of costs as well as health, but they can be considered only within the goals of the agency. Benefit-cost and risk-benefit are the most encompassing, although even they are not used in practice to address equity questions.

The second criterion is the intellectual foundation required of each framework. One can be most certain about the foundation for the simple frameworks, but drawing in additional considerations requires more knowledge, assumptions, and value judgments. The wider coverage comes at a price. In some cases there is insufficient knowledge to be able to quantify or even explore these other considerations; if so, there is no alternative to a simple framework or an ad hoc decision.

The third criterion is the resources required to implement the framework. The more complicated frameworks require exploration of further aspects of the problem, which in turn requires more data collection and analysis. Generally the resources available to analyze alternative regulations constitute a small proportion of those available for drafting and defending the regulations, and a minuscule proportion of the cost of carrying out the regulation. If additional analysis can result in even a tiny improvement in the quality of the regulation, the reduction in implementation and other costs should more than pay for the effort.

The fourth criterion is felicitousness. The world is complicated; it changes so rapidly that an agency rarely gets to second-order priority issues. The most important issues must be treated first, and they must be raised in easily comprehended fashion. If the issues are posed in a confused or obscure manner, the decision is likely to be made on an ad hoc basis. The felicitousness of the framework is more important than its comprehensiveness.

None of these frameworks is sufficiently complete and sound to serve as an automatic way of making decisions. The current Delaney Clause framework would appear to be the most concrete; even it, however, becomes mired in controversy over proving carcinogenicity—for example, the Newberne study regarding nitrite.[28]

The other frameworks have the more difficult task of quantifying risk and of attempting to quantify other aspects of the issue (for example, the value of greater choice). In all cases judgment is required to examine the suitability of the quantification, the factors that could not be quantified, and the valuation of the aspects that were quantified. These issues are far too complicated for a mechanical decisionmaking framework to be appropriate—for example, one of pursuing a project if and only if estimated benefits exceed costs.

The real question is the extent to which each of these frameworks can prove helpful in informing the decisionmaker. Must all effects be quantified accurately and all valuations be agreed upon before benefit-cost analysis is helpful?[29] If complete quantification is not possible or if there are difficulties in estimating risk, is it better to slip back to a less demanding framework, possibly back to the no-risk framework?[30] The answer depends on both the amount of uncertainty and the extent to which the general nature of the uncertainty is known. No analysis of health and safety regulations has managed to quantify all aspects of the issue, and it is evident that no future analysis can be expected to be complete. If this lack of completeness is deemed fatal, there is no point in considering benefit-cost analysis further.

28. Paul M. Newberne, "Dietary Nitrite in the Rat." See also Newberne, "Nitrite Promotes Lymphoma Incidence in Rats, pp. 1079–81; Council on Agricultural Science and Technology, "Comments on the Newberne Report on the Effect of Dietary Nitrite in the Rat"; *Food Safety and Quality,* Hearings, pp. 5–28, 176–80, 131–34, 236–38, 356–64; Comptroller General of the United States, *Does Nitrite Cause Cancer? Concerns about Validity of FDA-Sponsored Study Delay Answer.*

29. See, for example, Howard Raiffa, *Decision Analysis: Introductory Lectures on Choice under Uncertainty.*

30. For a discussion of this point see Richard Zeckhauser and Albert Nichols, "The Occupational Safety and Health Administration: An Overview," app., pp. 161–248; and National Academy of Sciences, *Decision Making for Regulating Chemicals in the Environment.*

Even partial quantification is helpful in making complicated decisions. Knowing that an effect is very important or of no importance is helpful in the analysis. Offsetting this contribution is the tendency of quantified effects to drive out ones that cannot be quantified, but it should be possible to recognize this tendency and attempt to correct it. Even where an effect cannot be quantified, knowing the nature of the effect can be sufficient. For example, the aesthetic effects of air pollution have not been quantified well and are unlikely to be for some time but the sign of the effect is known. Thus if a benefit-cost analysis finds that the quantified benefits exceed the costs, then adding aesthetic effects can only make the benefits even larger.[31] A more complicated example is spices. They contain toxic substances, including carcinogens, in minute quantities (for example, safarole). The risk of contracting cancer from the use of most spices in cooking food is minuscule and the enjoyment of better-tasting food is great. Should spices be banned in order to eliminate a tiny, controllable source of risk? In general some of the risks can be computed using standard techniques, but the benefits are more difficult to estimate.

The purpose of regulation is to lower risk or to attain some other social goal. Quantifying the benefits of a proposed or existing regulation is difficult, however. As illustrated in chapter 4, estimating health effects requires a number of assumptions. Quantifying effects on diversity of choice or consumer satisfaction is even more difficult, but any regulation requires at least an implicit estimate of these effects; they cannot be ignored.

In choosing a framework for each agency Congress has implicitly met social goals. For example, the market regulation framework keeps the government from regulating health and safety; only by providing facts and analyses can the government influence consumers and businesses. The no-risk framework sets a goal of reducing carcinogenicity without the complications of considering trade-offs among other social goals. Benefit-cost analysis implicitly elevates the importance of economic efficiency and downplays political and equity considerations. Selecting a decision framework is a crucial first step in deciding how to regulate health and safety. The importance of this choice is illustrated in the next two chapters in an examination of a series of regulatory decisions.

31. Lave and Seskin, *Air Pollution and Human Health,* p. 212; and U.S. Environmental Protection Agency, *Protecting Visibility: An EPA Report to Congress,* pp. 11-12 through 11-17.

CHAPTER THREE

Problems in Estimating the Consequences of Regulation

THE TWIN PURPOSES of analyzing social regulation are, first, to separate scientific issues from values or political consensus-building and, second, to trace out the implications of proposed actions. The former is important because scientific facts are the hard reality that condition political solutions; for example, not even a unanimous vote would stop gravity or change pi to 3.0. Ignoring scientific facts is attempting to govern by dreaming. Tracing out the implications of alternative policies allows poor policies to be identified and discarded.

A more subtle consequence of the use of an analytic framework is the prevention of an instant decision. The more contemplative approach requires the decisionmaker to step back from the problem, muster facts, identify alternatives, and examine consequences. The eight frameworks discussed in chapter 2 differ in the extent to which they serve these ends. Market regulation, no-risk, and technology-based alternatives are not analytic frameworks. Market regulation leaves the decision to consumers and producers and their individual frameworks and possible methods of analysis. No-risk provides an automatic reaction to a single piece of information concerning the existence of a risk; a single scientific fact is required and others are ignored along with any contemplation of alternatives or consequences. Similarly, technology-based standards attend to only one scientific fact (is there a viable technology that can reduce emissions or attain some other physical goal?); alternative proposals and consequences are ignored.

The previous chapter suggested some of the implications of using each framework to guide regulatory decisionmaking. These implications provide major criteria for evaluating the frameworks. The other major criterion is the ease of implementing each framework, from conceptual difficulties to time and professional resources required for each. The most important of these implementation difficulties are explored in this chapter, arranged (roughly) in the order they would arise in benefit-cost analysis (the most comprehensive framework). But the frameworks are sufficiently similar for some difficulties to be common. For example, the first two of the problems discussed arise in attempting to implement the no-risk framework, these plus the next arise for risk-risk, and so forth. Three general observations precede the discussion of these problems.

First, economists emphasize that resources are scarce and must be allocated carefully with attention to where they are most productive. Thus allocation of funds should be cost-effective (each additional set of resources should be allocated to the program where it will do the most to accomplish the goal). In practice, programs often coast on their reputations or past accomplishments, demanding resources because of past productivity or the average level of current productivity. Allocating resources by average productivity is a major mistake, since those programs lucky enough to have one or two really successful projects will commandeer resources for their weak siblings to the detriment of programs without such "superstar" projects.

Second, analysis must be incremental, constantly asking about the additional benefit to be gained from additional resources (and similarly asking about the magnitude of benefit to be lost from taking away some resources).

A third point is the difference between science and regulatory decision-making. Science is a timeless activity that seeks truth. Accuracy and completeness are more important than timeliness. If the state of knowledge concerning a particular program is such that confident predictions cannot be made, then scientists will eschew prediction until the knowledge base is more complete. In formulating public policy, timeliness is more important than completeness or even accuracy. The emphasis is on discovering the best possible answer, given the current state of knowledge and available time and resources. A reasonably good answer available for the formulation of policy is worth more than a perfect answer after a decision has been made and implemented. Social systems exhibit inertia; once a program is set in motion, changing its course and speed is difficult. Thus much is lost if a program starts off in a pernicious, or even irrelevant, direction.

The goals of science and policy analysis are often in conflict. Given the need for the latter to come to timely judgments, uncertainties abound. Although an experiment might conceivably resolve ambiguities or the progress of science might end the uncertainty, often a decision must be made immediately. In view of the extent and importance of uncertainties in policy analysis, remarkably little attention has been given to explicit explorations of their effects and how analysis and decision procedures can be improved in the face of ambiguities.[1]

Uncertainty stems not merely from the preliminary state of scientific knowledge of certain questions but also from inherently stochastic mechanisms and from the variability of public opinion. For example, the weather next year will be stochastic, and so an analysis of required stocks of heating fuel will always have an error band. Public attitudes change gradually with increases in income and changes in the age distribution of the population—for example, the desirability of government financing of medical care for the aged. Attitudes can change swifty when an event or a book, film, or other widely disseminated thought catalyzes shared reactions, as occurred for automobile safety. When dealing with uncertainty stemming from stochastic mechanisms or public attitudes, there is no substitute for careful, explicit modeling of the sources of variation in order to get estimates that will inform the decisionmakers.

Enumerating and Quantifying the Effects

The application of the decision frameworks raises questions about the ability to do quantitative analysis at all and, if the ability exists, the desirability of attempting to apply the more general frameworks. Analysis begins with an enumeration of the effects of some proposed project or regulation. In benefit-cost analysis this listing is intended to be encyclopedic, encompassing all nontrivial effects. The cost-effectiveness and the regulatory budget frameworks focus on the goal and on costs, attempting to find the cheapest way of accomplishing the goal, whereas in the no-risk and risk-risk frameworks, ill health is the only relevant effect.

The seemingly simple step of enumerating effects has often led to difficulties. For example, although the Army Corps of Engineers has been doing benefit-cost analyses of waterway projects since the 1930s, environmental effects were not considered explicitly until the late 1960s. While a more comprehensive listing is preferred, not all effects can be listed. Since the world is interdependent, an action will eventually have

1. See, however, Howard Raiffa, *Decision Analysis: Introductory Lectures on Choices under Uncertainty.*

ripple effects throughout a wide range of phenomena. Insisting on enumerating all effects would require a near infinite list; to make analysis tractable, most trivial effects must be excluded. Which effects are trivial is the heart of the controversy. Until the late 1960s the Corps of Engineers believed that environmental effects were trivial. Many people would think that threatening extinction of an obscure and not very desirable type of plant (for example, the furbish lousewort) would be a trivial effect, but a vocal minority disagrees emphatically.

The second step, relating the level of effect to the scope of the project or regulation, is necessary for each framework except no-risk and technology-based standards. For example, the cost of a crash-resistant bumper must be related to the extent of protection and the decrease in repair costs; improvements in air quality must be related to the decrease in the number of people becoming ill.

The greatest difficulty in applying an analytic framework is in this quantification of effects. Some effects cannot be measured with current data and analytic techniques. Unfortunately there is a Gresham's law of decisionmaking: quantified effects tend to dominate consideration, even if the other effects are believed to be more important. Since qualitative judgments are given far less attention than numerical estimates, quantification can be counterproductive if important aspects are unexplored, if the analysis is not evenhanded for benefits and costs, or if it is inadequate.

The Gresham's law problem can be alleviated in part by educating decisionmakers about the bias. Important aspects are certain to be unquantified, and so these frameworks will be helpful to decisionmakers only if they are educated about the nature of the biases and the ways in which effects have been estimated. A particular regulation problem is the universal quantification of costs and the absence of, or inadequate, estimation of benefits. Both benefit-cost and other quantitative analyses will be unable to quantify some effects that are important or of potential importance. There is no alternative to the education of decisionmakers about this problem.

Qualitative or vague estimates can be incorporated into the process. A vague estimate, such as "I think this substance could do enormous harm," can be quantified by estimating the likelihood of various levels of damage.[2]

2. National Academy of Sciences, *Analytical Studies for the U.S. Environmental Protection Agency*, vol. 2: *Decision Making in the Environmental Protection Agency*, pp. 31, 241–42; M. Granger Morgan, Max Henrion, and Samuel C. Morris, "Expert Judgements for Policy Analysis."

Using subjective estimates is both straightforward and proper, although the analyst must take pains to indicate the quality of each piece of information, especially when expert guesses are used. Techniques exist for eliciting subjective estimates and for reconciling the estimates of several people.

Qualitative judgments are among the most important. Is saccharin a human carcinogen? Would Congress enact legislation to ban it? When uncertainty dominates, parallel analyses can be conducted, one of which assumes that saccharin is not a carcinogen and one of which assumes it is. The loss associated with making the wrong decision, either by being overly cautious or not cautious enough, can be examined as well as the likelihood of each possibility.[3] The action that minimizes expected loss is likely to be one that assumes an unfavorable outcome (saccharin is a carcinogen) but is not hasty or dogmatic (curtail unnecessary and marginal uses of saccharin and work generally to lower exposure, but do not ban it immediately).

In order to estimate the quantitative relationship between the effects and scope of a project, data must be collected and analyzed. For some effects, such as the cost of constructing a building, techniques for quantifying the effects are well defined, accepted, and involve little controversy. As the example suggests, however, defined techniques are not synonymous with confident estimates, as evidenced by large budget overruns. At the opposite extreme from the cost of a building are health effects, which are difficult to estimate and which give rise to privacy issues.

To collect good data and to perform meaningful analyses requires a modicum of understanding of the underlying cause and effect relationship. Without this understanding, the data and analysis merely present empirical regularities. Physiological mechanisms, such as the effects of long-term exposure to low levels of some toxic substance, are not well understood; indeed, the quantitative effects on health of various exposures are generally obscure. Health effects are only one example of effects where the underlying theoretical knowledge is missing so that no one can specify precisely what data ought to be collected and how they ought to be analyzed.

Even when one knows which data to collect, acquiring them is difficult. For example, research on the effect of air pollution on health requires data on the quantities of various air pollutants breathed by an individual over

3. See, for example, Dennis Epple and Lester Lave, "Helium: Investments in the Future," pp. 617–50.

his lifetime; it further requires specifying the size and composition of the particulates and the form of the sulfur and nitrogen oxides. These data are difficult to obtain because of both measurement problems and the time span involved. Typically, available data are only a remote approximation to what is desired.

Rarely does theory or knowledge of the underlying mechanisms result in a sharp hypothesis to be tested. Instead, only vague statements of relationships are possible. This puts a premium on robust estimation procedures rather than on procedures whose power stems from a host of assumptions that cannot be derived from underlying theory or justified by previous empirical regularities.

Proving Causation

For chronic disease and accidents of low incidence, a significant problem is determining the cause. Data on human experience are most realistic, but sorting out confounding effects is difficult. Data from laboratory experiments are clearer with respect to causation, but difficulty arises in inferring the effects on people at observed doses. Often the choice is between human data of doubtful quality and experimental data of doubtful relevance.

Since human data are generally of poor quality and there is only vague knowledge of the theory or underlying mechanism, scientists often remark that a statistically significant relationship is not proof of a cause and effect relationship. Even where reverse causation (increased mortality does not cause air pollution) and chance relationships can be ruled out, there remains the possibility of spurious correlation, that is, the existence of some other factor or set of factors that causes both air pollution and mortality and thus leads to an association between the two.[4] The less well-founded the theory and the more vague the data, the more doubt scientists will have about whether the observed association is a causal one.[5]

This problem of spurious correlation also extends to the estimation of the quantitative effect. If relevant factors are missing from the analysis,

4. Herbert A. Simon, "Spurious Correlation: A Causal Interpretation," pp. 467–79.
5. Lester B. Lave and Eugene P. Seskin, "Epidemiology, Causality, and Public Policy," pp. 178–79.

and if they are correlated with those being analyzed, the latter will have biased parameter estimates.[6]

A special case of the general notion that some effects are easier to quantify than others is program costs versus health benefits. There are well-established methods of estimating the former, but estimating the latter is extremely difficult. Presenting decisionmakers with dollar estimates of costs and vague statements about benefits will lead them to reject good projects or regulations, at least during periods of economic difficulty.

Conservative versus Most Probable Estimates

Conservative interpretation of an analysis (the worst believable health effects) is often confused with estimates of the magnitude of the effect. Thus in order to arrive at a defensible estimate, it is general practice to use the most conservative, or at least a highly conservative, assumption whenever there is uncertainty.[7] Instead of producing a defensible estimate, however, this procedure merely produces a biased one that suppresses valuable information about the magnitude of the effect. An unintended result is to exaggerate effects most in those cases where there is the greatest ignorance. Thus this procedure allocates the most resources to the cases where there is the most uncertainty.

A far better procedure would be to identify at each stage (where there is uncertainty or randomness) a most probable estimate and lower- and upper-bound estimates. Employing the most probable estimate (or range of best estimates if no unique one can be identified) at each stage will produce a most probable overall estimate (or range of estimates); employing upper- and lower-bound estimates at each stage will produce a range of possible estimates. In order to give meaning to these upper- and lower-bound estimates, the probability of each estimate at each individual stage must be calculated and then used to deduce the probability that the lowest or highest estimate would occur at every stage. Alternatively,

6. In the extreme case, suppose $Y = a + bx + c$ and $\rho(x,w) = 1$. Then fitting $Y = a + bw + c$ will result in a statistically significant coefficient, even though Y is causally unrelated to w.

7. Lester B. Lave, "Air Pollution Damage: Some Difficulties in Estimating the Value of Abatement," p. 238.

where the difficulty results from uncertainty rather than randomness, the precise assumption that leads to each resulting estimate can be identified, with the hope that future work will show which assumption obtains.

Unfortunately current practice is to employ assumptions of various degrees of conservation at each stage to arrive at an overall estimate that is so muddled it cannot be interpreted beyond showing that it is conservative. The muddle is confounded when an even lower bound is estimated using more stringent assumptions. Presenting either or both of these estimates to a decisionmaker is misleading, even if they are termed "conservative." Displaying the upper and lower bounds is likely to be more enlightening. For example, if the range is zero to infinity and the extreme points are estimated to have probabilities of as large as 0.05, presenting a single estimate is misleading.

Aggregating Effects

The information gleaned in the enumeration and quantification stages is of importance and should always be reported, along with any further analysis. One framework (the sort of "effects" or "risks" analysis used by Raiffa and others) chooses to stop at this point, assuming that any aggregation of such diverse effects as morbidity, food appearance, and food prices is necessarily arbitrary and hinders understanding.[8] For example, the effects of abating pollution of the air by sulfur oxides would be described in terms of the number of tons of steel, man-hours for construction and maintenance, various other materials, and land needed for abatement, while the benefits would be described by estimated effects on disease and mortality rates, on visibility, odors, plants, animals, and so forth. Perhaps some people can make sense of such a collection of items, but most find it confusing.

All the frameworks (except no-risk and technologically-based standards) go on to aggregate effects to some extent, finding a common metric (at least within each category). Thus the inputs required to construct a project are aggregated by finding the cost of purchasing each in the market. As the example demonstrates, however, this step is not without controversy. The market value of land generally must be estimated amidst

8. Howard Raiffa, William B. Schwartz, and Milton C. Weinstein, "Evaluating Health Effects of Societal Decisions and Programs," pp. 1–81.

major uncertainty.[9] People often do not regard market value as reflecting the social cost of taking the land—for example, this value probably does not include the costs of flooding croplands or turning wilderness into suburbs. People may feel that the price of land ought to depend on whether it will be used as a park or open sewer. Aggregating health effects requires a sort of grisly calculus. A worsening of air pollution is estimated to increase the number of sick days, the amount of disability, and the mortality rate. Finding a metric to weight disabilities and premature deaths so they can be aggregated into a health effects category is inherently difficult.[10]

Risk-benefit, cost-effectiveness, and regulatory budget analyses stop when effects have been aggregated into major categories. Risk-benefit analysis attempts to aggregate the risks associated with a project on one side of the scale and the estimated benefits of the project on the other. If the risks are aggregated, the costs are included, the benefits are estimated, and the information is arrayed so that the benefits per unit of cost or risk are estimated—risk-benefit analysis is transformed into cost-effectiveness analysis. The basic assumption of that framework is that it is currently impossible to translate costs and benefits into comparable units, although overall costs can be estimated in dollars and benefits in some other unit. Thus the problem is set up as a constrained optimization: seek the greatest benefits for a given level of expenditure (or of risk).

Benefit-cost analysis assumes that all effects can be translated into the same metric. Thus rather than ending with estimates of the risk-benefit ratio or benefit per dollar of expenditure per project, the analysis produces an estimate of the relationship of benefits to costs. Being the most comprehensive of the frameworks, benefit-cost analysis is the focus of the criticism of quantitative analysis. The major problems are common to all these frameworks, however.

Separating the costs due to the regulation (or activity) from other costs is often difficult or impossible. Consider a new plant built with pollution control; how much of the cost should be ascribed to environmental controls? A large part of the project costs are planning, design, site acquisi-

9. For an extended discussion of this topic see A. Myrick Freeman III, *The Benefits of Environmental Improvement: Theory and Practice.*

10. Lester B. Lave and Warren E. Weber, "A Benefit-Cost Analysis of Auto Safety Features," pp. 265–75; Robert L. Berg, ed., *Health Status Indexes;* D. L. Patrick, J. W. Bush, and M. M. Chen, "Toward an Operational Definition of Health," pp. 6–23; and Robert H. Brook and others, *Conceptualization and Measurement of Health for Adults in the Health Insurance Study,* vol. 8: *Overview.*

tion, and other "overhead" items unrelated to the precise scope of the project. One estimate of environmental control costs would be to ask how much construction costs would be reduced if at the last moment the pollution control were eliminated. This estimate is likely to be low since it would involve saving only the costs of purchasing the pollution control equipment and putting it into place. None of the planning, design, or other costs would be reduced. But if the company desiring the plant had known at the earliest stages of planning that no pollution control would be required, they might have chosen a different site or production process, with much lower plant costs. In addition to this basic point about less expensive sites and planning, some portion of the design and other overhead costs should be attributed to pollution control. Obviously one extreme assumption is no more justified than the other. Overhead costs must be considered to be common or joint costs whose allocation is inherently arbitrary.

Estimating benefits is fraught with difficulties. Some items are not generally traded in the market and so carry no market price, for example, noxious odors in the air. Insuperable difficulties arise when the project is of a scale to produce changes in the prices of those items purchased and produced. When this occurs partial equilibrium analysis is no longer appropriate and the difficulties are many times greater.

Consumer Information and Decisionmaking

Consumer sovereignty provides a major part of the foundation of neoclassical economic theory. With the exception of children and those who are mentally incompetent, economists assume that consumers know what combination of goods and services will make them happiest. It is consumer sovereignty and the belief that companies engage in long-run profit maximization that support economists' faith in the marketplace and in the informational content of prices.

While both profit maximization and consumer sovereignty have been attacked, the latter is the focus of most current criticism. The controversy has shifted away from arguments that consumers cannot know what is best for them to arguments that they have insufficient information and knowledge to make the complicated choices among products. There can be no doubt of the multifaceted nature of the decision and of the underlying attributes; in reaching a decision the consumer must balance initial cost, expected lifetime, maintenance and operating costs, safety, and other attributes. Indeed the principal counterargument is that the questions are sufficiently complicated that there is no single best decision for all consumers. Economists point out that it is unnecessary for all consumers to be well informed; no company could stay in business making inferior or dangerous products because a few consumers would find the problem, stop buying the product, tell others, and perhaps sue for damages. Rumors of tainted cranberries or canned goods have ruined companies.[11]

Whether consumer sovereignty and discipline of the marketplace or its alternative of paternalism and regulation is deemed the appropriate description of the world is largely a philosophical issue, not an empirical one. On the one hand numerous examples can be produced of smart consumers who changed the market and of companies that managed to revolutionize their industry. On the other hand numerous examples can be produced of consumer stupidity and the venality of corporations. Each example of corporate stupidity can be matched with an example of regulatory stupidity.

Valuing Nontraded Goods: The Value of Life

Two issues have occupied much of the economic literature on benefit-cost analysis: the valuation of nontraded goods and services and the social rate of discount. Where some good is regularly bought and sold in the market and one can expect to be able to purchase the needed quantity without raising price, valuation is simple. But where the good or service is not normally bought or sold, such as life or health, valuation is difficult and fraught with controversy. Four options are possible in such cases. First, if these effects cannot be valued, cost-effectiveness is the appropriate framework. Second, entirely subjective judgments can be used to produce an analysis that is likely to be helpful only to the person making the judgments. Third, the traded good that is most similar to the untraded good can be found. For example, in choosing their occupation, sports, and other

11. "United States to Pay Indemnity for Cranberry Losses," *Science*, vol. 131 (April 8, 1960), pp. 1033–34; "Bon Vivant to Open under a New Name and Tight Controls," *New York Times*, November 14, 1972, p. 28; and Paul L. Montgomery, "Botulism Death in Westchester Brings Hunt for Soup," *New York Times*, July 2, 1971.

activities, people are implicitly trading costs, wages, convenience, and other factors against the risk of premature death. Fourth, people can be asked to think about the issue and make judgments. There is little agreement on the proper way of valuing such untraded effects, particularly where emotion enters, as with health.

The single most controversial aspect of benefit-cost analysis is the attempt to place a dollar value on averting a premature death. The attempt to do this may call to mind the cold-blooded sacrifice of persons whose death will grieve relatives and friends. Policy choices, however, result in a change in some mortality rates, such as an increase in the number of highway deaths. After a traffic policy has been in effect, accident statistics can be used to estimate the change in the number of deaths, but there is no way to identify which individuals were saved or killed by the decision.

A large literature on the cost of premature death documents a number of theoretical approaches and a number of numerical values used explicitly or implicitly in decisions concerning risk. For example, both the Department of Defense and state workers' compensation programs pay the heirs of a victim a sum of money.[12] While there is no notion that this payment is full compensation for the death, it nonetheless serves as a dollar estimate of the cost to society of premature death. In both cases the dollar values are quite low. The Federal Aviation Administration uses an explicit value of life of $300,000 in its various analyses.[13] They report that this figure results from recent court awards. The Nuclear Regulatory Commission places an implicit value of $1 million on premature death in its regulations concerning routine releases of radiation from nuclear power plants.[14] A large number of analyses have used values ranging from $40,000 to $80,000 based on the present discounted value of future earnings.[15] A number of studies of occupations have been done under the assumption that there is a premium associated with additional risk. These

12. For examples, see the Federal Employees Compensation Act, 5 U.S.C. 8133; and section 307 of the Pennsylvania Workmen's Compensation Law of 1950.

13. U.S. Department of Transportation, Federal Aviation Administration, *Establishment Criteria for Category I Instrument Landing System (ILS)*, p. B-8.

14. James G. Terrill, "Cost-Benefit Estimates for the Major Sources of Radiation," pp. 1008–13.

15. Barbara S. Cooper and Dorothy P. Rice, "The Economic Cost of Illness Revisited," p. 30; Lester B. Lave and Eugene P. Seskin, *Air Pollution and Human Health*, pp. 218–21, 348–49; and Joanne Linnerooth, "The Value of Human Life: A Review of the Models."

studies find a systematic wage premium associated with additional risk whose magnitude implies the expected value of a worker's life is between $260,000 and $2.1 million.[16]

The proper concept is the amount a person would be willing to pay (or would have to be paid for increased risk) to lower his probability of death by the prescribed amount. This individual payment must be supplemented by the additional loss that society suffers from the demise of this person, for example, the loss of his earning capacity to his family and the general loss to his family, employer, and community caused by his demise. There is no agreement on what dollar value best implements these concepts, but estimates in the range of $250,000 to $500,000 seem to be commonly used and defended. An important point is that the decision is rarely sensitive to the precise value chosen; formulation of the problem within a quantitative analysis framework is sufficient to distinguish between most programs that make sense and those that do not.[17]

Perhaps the most difficult untraded service to value is the aesthetic quality of the environment. How much is it worth to have more clear, sunny days? To be able to see ten miles instead of two? To have an atmosphere or lake that does not appear polluted and that does not have noxious odors? Researchers have quizzed people on the value of better visibility using a "bidding" framework to prevent obvious cheating.[18] People appear to value visibility highly.

The Social Rate of Discount

When effects accrue over many years they must be adjusted to make them commensurate in time. This is done by choosing a discount rate (which need not be constant over time). Economists have managed to resolve the theoretical issue concerning what discount rate to use: the opportunity cost of the funds invested in the project.[19] There is less agree-

16. Robert Stewart Smith, *The Occupational Safety and Health Act,* p. 91; Richard Thaler and Sherwin Rosen, "The Value of Saving a Life: Evidence from the Labor Market," pp. 265–98; and Linnerooth, "The Value of Human Life."

17. John D. Graham and James W. Vaupel, "The Value of Life: What Difference Does It Make?"

18. Robert D. Rowe, Ralph C. d'Arge, and David S. Brookshire, "An Experiment on the Economic Value of Visibility," pp. 1–19; David S. Brookshire, Berry C. Ives, and William D. Schulze, "The Valuation of Aesthetic Preferences"; and U.S. Environmental Protection Agency, *Protecting Visibility: An EPA Report to Congress.*

19. Baumol, "On the Social Rate of Discount."

ment, however, about the precise numerical value to use, since this depends in part on expectations concerning the future. Obtaining agreement on the numerical discount rate requires an estimation of what activities society will forgo in order to provide the funds to the project in question. Will private investment, government investment, current government expenditures, or current private consumption be curtailed? Knowledge of how the funds will be raised (for example, an increase in the income tax or a sale of long-term bonds) will yield some notion of the forgone opportunity. Secondary adjustments will take place, however, spreading the cost more widely.

Another conceptual problem is estimating the return that would be realized by the forgone investment. Estimates are available of the return on previous investments, or even on current investments, but the return over the next several years or decades is unknown. For the foreseeable future there is no possibility that a consensus will emerge on a precise number to be used as the discount rate. Best practice consists of carrying through the calculations with a range of discount rates, such as real (after inflation adjustment) rates of 2, 5, and 10 percent.[20]

The choice of a constant real discount rate assumes that the opportunity cost of invested funds will remain approximately constant over time, but the future could turn out much brighter or much worse. In principle there is no reason to use a constant discount rate. In practice analysts use a constant rate because they are unsure of what better assumption to make. Unless the path of future economic conditions seems fairly certain, anything other than a constant rate would be arbitrary, even though the most unlikely future was no change in economic conditions. Two conditions might lead to using a discount rate that changed systematically over time. First, if the future seemed to be growing ever brighter and if incomes were accelerating, the discount rate should be raised, causing less investment in the distant future and more current and near-term consumption.[21] Second, a future threatening falling rates of growth in income or falling incomes should prompt a lower, declining discount rate in order to induce additional investment that would have the effect of transferring consumption from the present to the future. For a risk-averse decisionmaker, the more uncertain the future, the lower the discount rate should

20. See, for example, Epple and Lave, "Helium," p. 5.
21. Raising the discount rate would tend to increase current consumption at the cost of investment, thus lowering future consumption.

be (at the more pessimistic end of the range) in order to ensure at least a minimum level of future consumption.

Although economics has been called the dismal science, economists generally envision the opposite of a Malthusian world, one in which society gets richer and richer and there is less concern about economic privation. Economists are among the most optimistic of futurists, forecasting that rates of productivity increase and of GNP growth comparable to that of the postwar period will prevail into the indefinite future.[22] If so, our children will be richer than we, and our grandchildren still more so. But productivity increases slowed in the late 1960s and stopped in the 1970s.[23] If recent economic history is conceived to be more than a temporary aberration, society should opt toward lower real discount rates.

Improved health in the future raises a new set of complicated issues. Consider a person being exposed to a substance that could produce cancer after a lag of twenty years. Getting cancer in twenty years is of less concern than getting it today. The victim might die of other causes in the meantime, making the cancer irrelevant, or a cure might be found. Even if neither situation occurs, the victim would have had twenty additional years of life. The present concern for getting cancer in twenty years will also be influenced by the general set of opportunities open to the person, including his wealth and income, the price of goods and services, and various risk-money or health-promoting money trade-off opportunities open to the person at that point.

This relatively simple question gives rise to others that are virtually unanswerable. Is it preferable for a forty-year-old to get cancer today or for someone who will be forty in twenty years to get cancer at that time? Presumably the answer is to delay the cancer for twenty years, even though different persons are involved. A new twist is added by comparing the forty-year-old with someone in the next generation who can play no part in the current decision. Is it fair for those alive today to enjoy themselves at the expense of imposing a health burden on people yet unborn? If we were confident that a cancer cure would be found, the answer would be

22. National Academy of Sciences, *Energy in Transition 1985–2010: Final Report of the Committee on Nuclear and Alternative Energy Systems*, pp. 102–15; and National Academy of Sciences, National Research Council, *Energy Modeling for an Uncertain Future: The Report of the Model Resource Group Synthesis Panel of the Committee on Nuclear and Alternative Energy Systems*, pp. 13–16.

23. Edward F. Denison, *Accounting for Slower Economic Growth: The United States in the 1970s.*

easy. Finally, there is a set of questions answered in ad hoc fashion by current policy but with unsatisfying answers. How preferable is it to prevent a death due to cancer rather than a death due to an accident? Is it preferable to save the life of a newborn baby, a child, a young adult, or a seventy-five-year-old?

The set of virtually unanswerable questions includes the discount rate used for future health states. Factors tending to lower the discount rate would be a young age at initial exposure and great personal concern for future health states. Factors tending to increase the discount rate would be a belief that medical research will be fruitful and a high probability of not surviving to contract the disease. Little of the uncertainty is resolved by economic variables. Instead, questions about the personal beliefs of individuals and their personal discounting of their future health states dominate.

An error made in many benefit-cost analyses involves the discounting of future untoward effects, such as premature mortality, to the present using the usual social rate of discount. Discounting future health effects at the standard rate makes sense only if there is a fixed transformation rate between dollars and health. Quite different factors affect the future levels of real income and medical knowledge, and so a fixed transformation seems unlikely.

In particular, analysts must find some surrogate for the required figures by introspection or by asking people questions about their perception of the disutility of contracting cancer at various ages. If the disutility of contracting cancer is assumed to be reasonably constant over time, people could be asked to estimate the dollar cost or value of avoiding cancer and then be asked for a discount rate or discount factor to get an estimate of the current value. Alternatively, they could be asked for the present disutility of contracting cancer now as well as in twenty years. Would people be able to give answers in which they would have confidence?[24]

The same sort of simplifying assumption occurs in treating other nonmonetary goods and services. For example, damage to wilderness areas, to stratospheric ozone, or to other environmental entities is discounted as if each were a corporation investment. The bias of this procedure is unclear, since the cost of repair might rise or fall over time. In cases with "irreversible damage," repair is prohibitively expensive within a short

24. Baruch Fischoff and others, "Approaches to Acceptable Risk."

period. Like health effects, a more satisfactory way of dealing with such efforts would be to inquire directly about the nature of trade-offs over time.

Conclusion

The derivation of quantitative estimates for the effects of proposed policies is fraught with conceptual and practical difficulties. The level of theoretical knowledge, amount of past scientific work, and amount of agreement will determine the range of uncertainty surrounding each estimate. If an important concept cannot be estimated well or if policy-makers refuse to accept certain assumptions, a full-blown benefit-cost analysis will be impossible. As the last chapter revealed, the various frameworks for regulation require different levels of knowledge and analysis. It is nonsensical to attempt to force all questions into the same framework. To do so would be to throw away valuable information for those issues that can be quantified more completely or to require arbitrary assumptions for those issues dominated by uncertainty. A careful tailoring of the regulatory framework to the amount of scientific knowledge and certainty and to the judgments that society is willing to make should help to improve the quality of analysis and of regulation.

CHAPTER FOUR

Food Additives

IN THIS CHAPTER and the next one I attempt to apply the eight decision frameworks to case studies of federal regulation and other federal government decisions. Each case begins with a review of the scientific facts and uncertainties, and then the decision frameworks are introduced. An attempt is made to specify the regulatory solution that would emerge from each framework, the data and analysis requirements, and the extent to which each framework raises the most important issues first and in a felicitous way.

Ingested substances, even such common ones as water and salt, are benign in small quantities and toxic in large quantities. Some combination of regulation and individual judgment is required to keep exposure to a harmless level. For example, the Food and Drug Administration regulates the level of filth permitted in food. Clearly, insect parts, animal excretion, and dirt do not add to the quality, palatability, or wholesomeness of the food. If the producer used additional resources, the levels of these foreign materials could be reduced, but the FDA tries to balance the aesthetic and health benefits of further reduction against the cost of achieving a more stringent standard. It would be nonsense to have a standard of no contaminating material or even one of no detectable contaminants. The failure of Congress or the FDA to set such standards is not evidence that they favor filth in food. The FDA is to be commended for using a framework that balances costs against benefits in setting these tolerance levels.[1]

This balancing is carried out in an arbitrary, or at least a vague, fashion. Criteria such as the effect on the availability of food are used to temper

---

1. Richard A. Merrill, "Regulating Carcinogens in Food: A Legislator's Guide to the Food Safety Provisions of the Federal Food, Drug, and Cosmetic Act," pp. 245–46; Peter Barton Hutt, "Food Regulation," pp. 521–24, 533; and Richard A. Merrill, "Federal Regulation of Cancer-Causing Chemicals," chap. 2: "FDA Regulation of Environmental Contaminants."

zero risk in setting tolerance levels.[2] The exception is food additives that are known or suspected carcinogens; these additives now are prohibited without regard to offsetting benefits.

Although the FDA and the food industry have evolved a working system for toxic additives and contaminants, it involves great effort and long delays. Benefits are considered in a tortuous way, judgments are not uniform across substances, and the process is less than a systematic, objective one. The failure to consider the offsetting benefits of carcinogens leads to intense controversies, as with nonnutritive sweeteners.

People have stronger feelings about carcinogens, mutagens, and teratogens than about most other toxic substances, although only a small fraction of chemicals have been shown to be in these categories.[3] One expression of these strong feelings is the Delaney Clause (see note 2, chapter 2), which requires the FDA to ban food additives found to be carcinogenic and to prohibit carcinogens from being administered to animals if they leave a detectable residue in meat and other foods.[4]

A major controversy focuses on the number of carcinogens.[5] If many additives are carcinogenic, it would be impossible, or at least prohibitively expensive, to ban them. If few are, banning might not be expensive.

Believing that the risk of contracting cancer can be lowered to zero is simplistic. Increasing longevity guarantees that cancer will be a major cause of death. Furthermore, chemicals in the environment and many of our personal habits (for example, cigarette smoking) promote cancer. Rather than concentrating on food additives, it behooves regulators to look more generally at how they can lower the risks of cancer while still achieving their other goals. It makes no sense to press forward against

2. Merrill, "Regulating Carcinogens in Food," pp. 188, 190–91, 200.

3. See National Academy of Sciences, *Food Safety Policy: Scientific and Societal Considerations*, p. 9-6; J. Kendall and D. Kriebe, "Carcinogen File: The Ames Test," p. 15; and Interagency Regulatory Liaison Group, "Scientific Bases for Identifying Potential Carcinogens and Estimating Their Risks," p. 12.

4. See discussion in NAS, *Food Safety Policy*, apps. B and C; and Merrill, "Regulating Carcinogens in Food," pp. 175–84. Other parts of the Federal Food, Drug and Cosmetic Act of 1938, as amended, also attempt to keep toxic materials out of the food supply and other substances to which humans are exposed.

5. For a discussion of the debate see "Identification, Classification, and Regulation of Potential Occupational Carcinogens," *Federal Register*, vol. 45 (January 22, 1980), pp. 5028–29; and statement of Sidney Wolfe in *National Cancer Program, 1979*, Hearings before the Subcommittee on Health and Scientific Research of the Senate Committee on Labor and Human Resources, 96 Cong. 1 sess. (Government Printing Office, 1979), p. 195.

one aspect, such as food additives, while ignoring other aspects that pose greater risks.

Supporters of the current regulatory framework argue that, while eliminating cancer is impossible, risks that are controllable should be eliminated. Food additives are both easily controlled and of recent origin; such food contaminants as mercury and polychlorinated biphenyls (PCBs) are virtually impossible to control, and natural carcinogens have always been present in food. Simplicity of control, ease of administration, and length of experience are all reasons to treat similar substances differently.[6] Cost, including the cost of forgone opportunities, must be considered too.

Sodium Nitrite

Sodium nitrite is a salt used as a preservative for cured meats; it changes the color and flavor of meats and inhibits the growth of bacteria, particularly *Clostridium botulinum,* which produces one of the most potent known toxins and causes a frequently fatal type of food poisoning: botulism.[7] Salt has been used to preserve meats for thousands of years. Nitrate compounds are a contaminant of ordinary salt (sodium chloride) and are converted to nitrites by bacteria. The effect of salt on meat color and flavor was recognized as early as Roman times; the bacterial inhibition properties were recognized more recently. When added under controlled conditions, nitrite is extremely effective in controlling *C. botulinum;* no death due to botulism from cured meats has been reported in the United States for several decades, although a number of cases have been attributed to smoked fish, frozen foods, and canned meat or fish.[8]

Unfortunately nitrite is known to combine with amines and amides to produce nitrosamines, which are found to be potent carcinogens in animals.[9] Also, there is evidence that nitrite itself may be a carcinogen.[10]

6. Richard A. Merrill, "Saccharin: The Regulatory Context," in Robert W. Crandall and Lester B. Lave, eds., *The Scientific Basis of Health and Safety Regulation.*
7. See U.S. Food and Drug Administration and U.S. Department of Agriculture, "FDA's and USDA's Action Regarding Nitrite."
8. U.S. Department of Health, Education, and Welfare, Center for Disease Control, *Botulism in the United States 1899–1977: Handbook for Epidemiologists, Clinicians and Laboratory Workers,* pp. 35–41.
9. D. D. Fine and others, "N-Nitroso Compounds in Air and Water"; Steven R. Tannenbaum, "Relative Risk Assessment of Various Sources of Nitrite"; Donald C. Harvey and others, "Survey of Food Products for Volatile N-Nitrosamines," p. 540; R. Preussmann and others, "Dose-Response Study with N-Nitrosopyrrolidine and Some Comments on Risk Evaluation of the N-Nitroso Compounds," pp. 261–68.
10. Paul M. Newberne, "Dietary Nitrite in the Rat."

Thus the issue can be stated simply. Nitrite is valuable in controlling *C. botulinum* but is itself a carcinogen or is converted into a carcinogen. If nitrite were prohibited as a food additive and no other preservative were substituted, cases of botulism would probably increase, with resulting illness and death. While higher standards in meat processing would lower the concentration of *C. botulinum,* it would be impossible to eliminate all spores. The question can be stated starkly: If cured meats are not banned, banning nitrite would condemn some people to death, and not banning it also would condemn some people to death. Should nitrite be banned or required in cured meat? Should it be used in lesser amounts? Should its use be phased out as soon as "acceptable" substitutes can be found?

The Risks of Nitrosamines

The reaction of nitrites with amines and amides to form nitrosamines can occur in stored food, during cooking, or within the body.[11] The reaction is inhibited by the presence of vitamin C (sodium ascorbate, isoascorbate) and perhaps vitamin E (tocopherol).[12]

Nitrosamines are extremely potent carcinogens; for example, 100 micrograms of dimethylnitrosamine a day for 30 days caused liver tumors in 30–40 percent of rats.[13] Animal bioassay evidence seems conclusive, even at low concentrations. Human epidemiological evidence is almost impossible to obtain, even conceptually. Since nitrosamines are also produced within the body, even a good measurement of ingested nitrosamines would be only a partial indication of dose. Thus estimation of the risk to humans must solve three problems. First, the effective (internal) dose must be estimated. Measuring the actual dose of nitrosamines the rats received is impossible, since much is produced within their bodies. Similarly, the increase in nitrosamine dose for humans is in addition to that pro-

11. Fine and others, "N-Nitroso Compounds in Air and Water"; Tannenbaum, "Relative Risk Assessment"; Harvey and others, "Survey of Food Products for Volatile N-Nitrosamines"; Preussman and others, "Dose-Response Study with N-Nitrosopyrrolidine"; *Food Safety and Quality: Nitrites,* Hearings, pp. 286–303; and William Lijinsky, "Current Concepts in the Toxicology of Nitrates, Nitrites, and Nitrosamines," p. 157.

12. American Meat Institute, "The Effect of Alpha-Tocopherol on Nitrosamine Formation during Frying of Bacon"; and Lijinsky, "Current Concepts in the Toxicology of Nitrates, Nitrites, and Nitrosamines," p. 161.

13. William Lijinsky, "Health Problems Associated with Nitrites and Nitrosamines," p. 308.

duced within the body; some or most of the nitrosamines ingested may even have been produced within the body from nitrogen compounds in food through digestion.[14] Second, there must be extrapolation from the relatively high levels of nitrosamines fed laboratory animals to low levels. Third, there must be an extrapolation from rats to humans, assuming it is valid to extrapolate between these species.

The problem in extrapolating from lower animals to humans is difficult.[15] Differences in physiology mean that extrapolation cannot be done with confidence. Indeed, many scientists refuse to extrapolate quantitatively.[16] If an extrapolation is to be made, however, the usual procedure is to do it on the basis of dose per unit of body weight, for example, nanograms per kilogram. This extrapolation probably gives a rough indication of what might be expected. Dose per unit of surface area and equal concentrations in air, water, or diet for rats and humans are also used.

The second problem, estimating the effects of very low doses from the observed effects at high doses, is equally difficult.[17] Strictly speaking, it requires knowledge, rarely available, of the underlying mechanism by which the substance causes cancer or other adverse effects. The classic dose-response relationship from pharmacology is an S curve, indicating that some people are extremely sensitive to the substance and others are highly resistant.[18] This classic curve gives rise to the hypothesis that the dose-response function can be approximated by a probit curve in the low

14. Steven R. Tannenbaum and others, "Nitrite and Nitrate Are Formed by Endogenous Synthesis in the Human Intestine," pp. 1487–88; and S. S. Mirvish, "Formation of N-Nitroso Compounds: Chemistry, Kinetics, and *in vivo* Occurrence," p. 325.

15. U.S. Department of Health, Education, and Welfare and the National Institutes of Health, *Human Health and the Environment: Some Research Needs,* pp. 434–38; NAS, *Food Safety Policy,* pp. 13–14; D. G. Hoel, "Statistical Models for Estimating Carcinogenic Risks from Animal Data"; and Hoel, "Human Risk Assessment Based on Laboratory Animal Studies."

16. Gio Batta Gori, "The Regulation of Carcinogenic Hazards," pp. 256–61; J. L. Radomski, "Evaluating the Role of Environmental Chemicals in Human Cancer," p. 27; and memorandum, Arthur C. Upton, director of the National Cancer Institute, to the commissioner of the Food and Drug Administration, "Quantitative Risk Assessment."

17. D. G. Hoel, "Statistical Extrapolation Methods for Estimating Risks from Animal Data," pp. 418–20.

18. See Lester B. Lave and Eugene P. Seskin, *Air Pollution and Human Health,* pp. 44–48. The S curve also refers to the dose required to produce a heightened effect in an individual, such as the amount of an analgesic required to produce successively greater effects.

dose range.[19] Thus one of the most widely used procedures for estimating the effect of low doses is the Mantel-Bryan procedure for extrapolation.[20] Alternative models include logistic, multihit, and generalized log-probit.

An alternative approach notes that no effect can occur when the dose is zero and seeks to estimate the effect of a low dose by a linear extrapolation from a positive dose-response observation to zero; this approach assumes a "one-hit," or cumulative, model of occurrence.[21] In a one-hit model any molecule of the substance is regarded as having the same probability of causing the reaction; thus cumulative exposure will determine the cumulative probability of the response.

The choice of extrapolation procedure can be critical. The linear, no-threshold approach can predict a response will occur at a dose more than one hundred times smaller than would be predicted by the Mantel-Bryan approach in the low-dose region.[22] Knowledge of the physiological mechanisms involved can direct the choice of extrapolation procedure. Since this knowledge is rarely present, the choice is more often dictated by risk aversion and the extent of possible loss should the undesired effect occur.

Effects are also estimated by relating the length of time between exposure and the occurrence of the tumor to the dose level.[23] Generally this interval is an inverse function of dose. Thus for very low doses, not only would the estimated number of cancers be small, but they would not be expected to occur during a normal life span.

For some substances—for example, diethylstilbestrol—the extrapolation procedure from animals to humans is known to corroborate human

19. N. Mantel and W. R. Bryan, "Safety Testing of Carcinogenic Agents," pp. 455–70.

20. Ibid.; and N. Mantel and others, "An Improved Mantel-Bryan Procedure for 'Safety' Testing of Carcinogens," pp. 865–72.

21. The one-hit dose-response curve is an exponential that is approximately linear at low doses. HEW and NIH, *Human Health and the Environment*, pp. 77–84; Kamta Rai and John Van Ryzin, "Risk Assessment of Toxic Environmental Substances Using a Generalized Multi-Hit Dose Response Model," p. 102; and K. S. Crump, "Estimating Human Risks from Drug Feed Additives," pp. 27–28.

22. U.S. Office of Technology Assessment, *Drugs in Livestock Feed,* vol. 1: *Technical Report,* pp. 51–53.

23. See the review in David W. Gaylor and Raymond E. Shapiro, "Extrapolation and Risk Estimation for Carcinogenesis," pp. 81–85; plus Otto G. Raabe, Steven A. Book, and Norris J. Parks, "Bone Cancer from Radium: Canine Dose Response Explains Data for Mice and Humans," pp. 61–64; and H. B. Jones and A. Grendon, "Environmental Factors in the Origin of Cancer and Estimation of the Possible Hazard to Man," pp. 251–68.

experience.[24] A linear, no-threshold dose-response curve seems to fit some substances, for example, ionizing radiation.[25] Furthermore, there are substances that violate both extrapolation procedures, for example, benzene and arsenic.[26] Clearly one can have less confidence in estimates if both extrapolations must be made.

Green has done an extrapolation for nitrosopyrrolidine, which is formed when bacon is fried at high temperatures, and based on data from animal bioassays has roughly calculated the risk to humans of consuming bacon with 10 parts per billion of nitrosopyrrolidine.[27] Assuming that every American weighs 70 kilograms (155 pounds) and consumes 4 strips (1 ounce) of fried bacon a day, the expected number of cancers would be zero per year for a Mantel-Bryan extrapolation and eight for a linear extrapolation. Even the latter figure is so small that it could never be detected empirically; indeed, it is so small that minor changes in the extrapolation procedure, for example, using the Mantel-Bryan extrapolation rather than the linear one, could lower the estimate to zero. If people consumed 5 percent of that amount, linear extrapolation would predict 0.4 cancers a year. A similar risk calculation was carried out by the American Meat Institute, which estimated that nitrosopyrrolidine in bacon could lead to 0–24 cancers a year.[28] Risk estimates have not been done for other nitrosamines, primarily because of ignorance about human exposures.[29] Although the estimates above are an admirable tour de force, one can have little confidence in them. They are crude, not only because of the triple problems, but also because exposures to other compounds are rarely considered. These other chemicals might enhance the potency of nitrosopyrrolidine, be potentiated by it, or interact in other ways. The

24. George H. Gass, Don Coats, and Nora Graham, "Carcinogenic Dose-Response Curve to Oral Diethylstilbestrol," pp. 971–77.

25. National Academy of Sciences, *The Effects on Populations of Exposures to Low Levels of Ionizing Radiation;* Jones and Grendon, "Environmental Factors in the Origin of Cancer," pp. 255. See also S. Weinhouse, "Problems in the Assessment of Human Risk of Carcinogenesis by Chemicals," pp. 1307–10, for chemical carcinogens as well.

26. Both substances are human carcinogens, but at least until recently, neither has been found to be carcinogenic in any experimental animal system. See HEW and NIH, *Human Health and the Environment,* p. 362; and Thomas R. Bartman, "Benzene."

27. Laura Green, "A Risk/Risk Analysis for Nitrite," pp. 23–29.

28. American Meat Institute, "Assessment of Risks from Nitrosopyrrolidine and *Clostridium botulinum* in Bacon."

29. Tannenbaum, "Relative Risk Assessment."

value of the estimate is not the specific number, but the likelihood that fewer than one hundred deaths a year are caused by current exposure to nitrosopyrrolidine.

The Risks of Nitrite Itself

Shank and Newberne suggested that nitrite itself might be a carcinogen.[30] Thus the FDA commissioned an elaborate study using 2,244 rats in 18 groups to test the carcinogenicity of nitrite.[31] The results are generally positive, showing that rats exposed to high levels of nitrite had significantly more lymphomas than rats in control groups. There is little or no relationship, however, between the level of nitrite in the diet and the proportion of rats with cancer. Indeed, in some groups the proportion of rats with cancer falls as the dose increases. For example, 7.8 percent of rats not exposed to nitrite developed lymphomas, while lymphomas occurred in 14.7 percent exposed at 1,000 parts per million and 11.4 percent exposed at 2,000 parts per million. The increased lymphoma rate in going from zero to 1,000 parts per million is significant. In addition, questions have been raised about interpretation of the slides and the experimental procedures, including the care with which data were recorded and whether rats were always given the correct diets.[32]

The slides from the Newberne study were reviewed by a panel of pathologists who disagreed with many of the original classifications.[33] Their reclassification, including assigning many slides to a type of cancer that cannot be induced by nitrite, led to a conclusion that nitrite did not induce a significant increase in the lymphoma rate in rats.[34] Newberne, quoted as praising the care with which the work was reviewed, maintains his conclusion that nitrite led to a significant increase in lymphoma in the rats.[35]

30. R. C. Shank and Paul M. Newberne, "Dose-Reponse Study of Carcinogenity of Dietary Sodium Nitrite Morpholine in Rats and Hamsters," pp. 1–8. See also *Food Safety and Quality: Nitrites,* Hearings, pp. 131–32.

31. Newberne, "Dietary Nitrite in the Rat." See also FDA and USDA, "FDA's and USDA's Action Regarding Nitrite," p. 4.

32. See Council on Agricultural Science and Technology, "Comments on the Newberne Report on the Effect of Dietary Nitrite in the Rat."

33. U.S. Food and Drug Administration, *Re-evaluation of the Pathology Findings of Studies on Nitrite and Cancer: Histologic Lessons in Sprague Dawley Rats;* and FDA, *Report of the Interagency Working Group on Nitrite Research.*

34. FDA, *Report of the Interagency Working Group on Nitrite Research.*

35. R. Jeffrey Smith, "Nitrites: FDA Beats a Surprising Retreat," p. 1101.

The FDA, accepting the conclusion of the review panel, terminated its proposal to eliminate nitrite additives over time.[36]

The data from a single experiment, even one as elaborate as Newberne's, cannot be considered conclusive from a scientific viewpoint. A study involving many hundreds of animals over several years inevitably will raise questions about the experimental procedure and the interpretation of tissues. Furthermore, there is a natural rate of cancer in the animals and it is possible that chance or uncontrolled factors produced the effects that were found.[37] Replication by another investigator would be necessary to deal with many of the issues. The lack of a graduated response with increase in dose is troublesome. While it might only be the result of random variation, it could suggest some unrecognized complication or difficulty in experimental technique. Additional research is needed to reexamine the carcinogenicity of nitrite, even though it would be costly and time-consuming.

The FDA estimated the risk of contracting lymphomas from consuming nitrite in cured meat on the basis of Newberne's study.[38] Assuming people eat 1.6 ounces a day of cured meat containing 200 parts per million of nitrite (a high estimate), a linear, no-threshold extrapolation from Newberne's group showing the greatest sensitivity would imply 157–709 cancers a year. Since cured meat accounts for a range of 2–20 percent of total nitrite consumed, one can infer that the total nitrite dose would be estimated to cause 885–39,830 cancers a year.[39] The latter corresponds to an annual lymphoma rate of 0.41–18.6 per 100,000 population. But the actual incidence of lymphomas is about 11 per 100,000 a year.[40] Thus this extrapolation implies that nitrite causes between 3.7 and 169.1 percent of the lymphomas, assuming that the Newberne estimates are correct.

This FDA risk estimate not only is inconsistent with the incidence of lymphomas but is suspicious in itself. The Newberne study does not show that lymphomas increase linearly with dose.[41]

36. U.S. Food and Drug Administration, press release, August 19, 1980.

37. Newberne, "Dietary Nitrite in the Rat."

38. FDA and USDA, "FDA's and USDA's Action Regarding Nitrite," pp. 24–27.

39. Ibid., pp. 25–26A; and Food Safety and Quality: Nitrites, Hearings, p. 54.

40. Data are from the National Cancer Institute and are for 1976, male and female combined, age-adjusted to the 1970 population.

41. The possibility exists that the highest dose level will lead to acute toxicity and death before the tumor can develop. Interpretation of animal bioassays is fraught with difficulty.

The Benefits of Adding Nitrite to Cured Meats

As noted earlier, sodium nitrite inhibits the growth of *C. botulinum,* an anaerobic bacteria that is widely dispersed in the soil and even in the bodies of animals.[42] Under warm, airtight conditions the spores will generate, with the growing bacteria producing toxins that are poisonous in minute amounts. The distribution of spores in meat is random, with some pieces having high concentrations and others being almost spore free. When incubated at a temperature of about 80 degrees Fahrenheit, meat with large numbers of spores (10,000 per gram) will produce lethal amounts of the toxin within six hours; concentrations of 200–500 spores per gram will require about three days.[43] There are various strains of *C. botulinum,* some of which continue to grow down to temperatures of about 38 degrees.[44] To ensure the safety of tightly packed, spore-laden meats, they must be kept below 38 degrees Fahrenheit when stored, which is colder than most home refrigerators.[45] It is likely that meats cured without nitrite would have to be shipped, sold, and stored in a frozen state.

Since nitrite is so effective in controlling *C. botulinum,* cured meats are treated casually now, with canned hams left unrefrigerated and luncheon meats and frankfurters kept in the refrigerator for weeks. Without the protection of nitrite in cured meats, botulism could become a common disease causing many deaths. More likely are attempts to change consumer's habits through education, but one can only guess at how many people would not be reached, would forget, or would otherwise fail to act prudently.

Until recently nitrite was added to cured meats in much higher concentrations.[46] Until the 1920s nitrate as well as nitrite was added to meat, and bacterial action converted the nitrate to nitrite. Furthermore, little was known about the amount of nitrite sufficient to control *C. botulinum,* and it was difficult to spread the nitrite uniformly throughout the cured meat.

42. *Food Safety and Quality: Nitrites,* Hearings, p. 50; and FDA and USDA, "FDA's and USDA's Action Regarding Nitrite," p. 5.
43. *Food Safety and Quality: Nitrites,* Hearings, p. 60.
44. Ibid., p. 49.
45. Ibid., p. 100.
46. Comptroller General of the United States, *Does Nitrite Cause Cancer? Concern about the Validity of FDA-Sponsored Study Delay Answer,* pp. 2, 8–9; and Council on Agricultural Science and Technology, *Nitrite in Meat Curing: Risks and Benefits,* pp. 5, 6, 8.

Thus much larger quantities were added to ensure protection. Department of Agriculture regulations now limit the amount of nitrites to the levels needed to control *C. botulinum* growth (about 120–180 parts per million).[47]

In addition to protecting against botulism, sodium nitrite adds color and flavor to cured meats. Nitrite turns cured meats (which otherwise would be gray-brown) pink; about 40 parts per million are required to impart color.[48] Nitrite helps to give the distinctive flavors to ham, corned beef, and other cured meats; for example, without nitrite, bacon would be simply salt pork.[49] The flavor of cured meats is judged to improve with concentrations of up to at least 100 parts per million.[50] Higher concentrations are needed for *C. botulinum* protection; 120–170 parts per million will inhibit the growth of even concentrated spores for three weeks or longer.[51]

Prohibiting the addition of nitrite to cured meat would result in a product judged less palatable by consumers, who currently choose bacon and corned beef over salt pork and pickled beef. While consumers might change their tastes in response to new products and advertising, it is safe to presume that they would be willing to pay a great deal to satisfy their current tastes.

Lowering the Risk from Nitrite

Cured meat is but one of many sources of nitrite.[52] Nitrate, which is present in many foods, especially leafy vegetables, is converted to nitrite by bacteria in the human body. Furthermore, evidence shows that substantial quantities of nitrite are produced in the digestive process. Finally, nitrite itself is present in high concentrations in vegetables such as spinach. Tannenbaum has estimated that only about 3 percent of nitrite in the body comes from cured meats; about 15 percent comes from the saliva and

---

47. FDA and USDA, "FDA's and USDA's Action Regarding Nitrite," p. 4.

48. *Food Safety and Quality: Nitrites,* Hearings, p. 49.

49. CAST, *Nitrite in Meat Curing,* p. 13.

50. American Meat Institute, "Summary of Recent Research on Nitrite as It Relates to Botulinal Protection in Cured Meats," p. 14.

51. J. C. Bard and Oscar Meyer and Co., "Collaborative USDA, FDA, and AMI Studies on Sodium Nitrate and Sodium Nitrite in Cured Meat Products"; and *Food Safety and Quality: Nitrites,* Hearings, pp. 52–53.

52. See Tannenbaum, "Relative Risk Assessment," for a discussion of the various sources of nitrite.

about 82 percent comes from digestion.[53] Thus even if nitrite were eliminated from cured meats, there would be relatively little effect on total exposure. Indeed, much more could be done to lower nitrite exposure by changing the diet than by changing the level of nitrite in cured meats.[54]

No single compound offers the properties of sodium nitrite. Substances have been proposed for color, flavor, and inhibition of *C. botulinum,* but none of them has undergone extensive testing for toxicity, especially of the sort that nitrite has undergone through thousands of years of usage.[55] Care should be taken before substituting an unknown compound for nitrite. For example, Tris was added as a fire retardant in children's sleepware without adequate testing; although the chemical protected children against fire, it was found to be a carcinogen that could be absorbed through the skin.[56]

While no compound substitutes for nitrite, some compounds enhance its effects so that less can be used. Potassium sorbate has the effect of lowering the required concentration to inhibit *C. botulinum* by more than 50 percent.[57] It offers the hope of lowering the dose people get without lowering botulism protection. Adding vitamins C and E (which inhibit nitrosamine formation) to cured meats, as well as compounds such as potassium sorbate, which enhances the effect of nitrite, offers the hope of lowering exposure to both nitrite and nitrosamines.

Diethylstilbestrol as a Cattle Growth Stimulant

Diethylstilbestrol (DES) is a synthetic estrogen used as a drug for humans and, until recently, as a growth stimulant for cattle. Estrogens are used in the treatment of such conditions as gonadal dysgenesis and postmenopausal osteoporosis in women and prostate cancer in men. DES is used as a "morning after" drug to prevent pregnancy and was used un-

53. Ibid., p. 2.
54. The proportion of nitrite due to cured meats is generally stated to be 2–20 percent, as discussed above.
55. *Food Safety and Quality: Nitrites,* Hearings, pp. 52–53.
56. Robert H. Harris, "The Tris Ban," p. 1132; Philip H. Abelson, "The Tris Controversy," p. 113; and Arlene Blum and Bruce N. Ames, "Flame-Retardant Additives as Possible Cancer Hazards," pp. 17–23.
57. F. J. Ivey and others, "Effect of Potassium Sorbate on Toxinogenesis of *Clostridium botulinum* in Bacon"; and *Food Safety and Quality: Nitrites,* Hearings, pp. 52–53.

successfully to prevent miscarriage.[58] In the latter use the large doses were shown to be teratogenic and probably to cause cancer in the fetus.[59]

After nearly a decade of controversy, FDA has banned DES as a growth stimulant for cattle and other animals, both as an implant and as a feed supplement.[60] Unlike the case of sodium nitrite, there is no direct health benefit from using DES as a feed supplement. Thus the FDA's action seemed inevitable, delayed only by congressional intervention.

The Risks of DES for Humans

Human exposure to large doses of DES has come in three ways: exposure to DES as a drug, occupational exposure, and through accidents such as inadvertently putting DES into vitamins.[61] All three exposures have resulted in unfortunate consequences.

In the late 1940s and early 1950s large doses of DES were given to pregnant women believed to be at high risk of miscarriage, for example, those with histories of miscarriage. The large doses have been found to be teratogenic. About 90–95 percent of females exposed as fetuses show some genital abnormality such as ridges in the vagina or cervix.[62] The genital abnormalities disappear over time in most women.[63] Occupational expo-

58. Lucile K. Kuchera, "Postcoital Contraception with Diethylstilbestrol—Updated," pp. 47–55.

59. A. L. Herbst, "Summary of the Changes in the Human Female Genital Tract as a Consequence of Maternal Diethylstilbestrol Therapy," pp. 13–20; Herbst, "Written Testimony in the Matter of Diethylstilbestrol," FDA Docket No. 76 N-0002 (March 1977); Marluce Bibbo, "Final Progress Report on Contract NIH No. 1-4-2850"; and Bernard Kliman, "Testimony in the Matter of Diethylstilbestrol: Withdrawal of Approval of New Animal Drug Applications."

60. U.S. Food and Drug Administration, "Initial Decision: Proposal to Withdraw Applications for Diethystilbestrol."

61. R. M. Watrous and R. T. Olsen, "Diethylstilbestrol Absorption in Industry: A Test for Early Detection as an Aid in Prevention," pp. 469–72; C. Pagani, "Sindromi iperstriniche de origine esogena osservazioni in lavoratori addetti alla sintesi di sostanze estrogene e quadri sperimentali sull'animale," p. 1173; M. P. Fitzsimons, "Gynaecomastia in Stilbestrol Workers," p. 235; M. A. Goldzieher and J. W. Goldzieher, "Toxic Effects of Percutaneously Absorbed Estrogens," p. 1156; and Roy Hertz, "Accidental Ingestion of Estrogens by Children," pp. 203–06.

62. Arthur L. Herbst, Robert E. Scully, and Stanley J. Robboy, "The Significance of Adenosis and Clear Cell Adenocarcinoma of the Genital Tract in Young Females," p. 10.

63. Donald A. Antonioli, Louis Burke, and Emanuel A. Friedman, "Natural History of Diethylstilbestrol-Associated Genital Tract Lesions: Cervical Ectopy and Cervicovaginal Hood," pp. 847–53.

sure to DES was found to be a problem almost immediately after commercial manufacturing was begun. Men experienced gynecomastia, enlargement of the breasts, and sexual difficulties, but a combination of careful controls to limit exposure and periodic testing of workers (who may be switched to other jobs if they have developed abnormalities) have eliminated any observable symptoms. The possibility of problems occurring over the long term remains, however. Children exposed to DES that inadvertently found its way into vitamin pills through inadequately cleaned manufacturing equipment displayed gynecomastia. When the problem was discovered and exposure to DES was discontinued, the symptoms gradually subsided, although long-term damage cannot be ruled out.

DES is associated with clear cell adenocarcinoma, a potent cancer resulting in death in about 20 percent of the cases. The carcinogenic effects of DES were recognized in spite of the low incidence of the effects (approximately 0.14 to 1.4 per 1,000 women aged twenty-four or younger, who were exposed to DES in utero) because clear cell adenocarcinoma is extremely rare.[64] Of the 250 cases of adenocarcinoma in the registry in 1977, two-thirds of those stricken were known to have been exposed to DES in utero.[65] Others may have received drugs that were not recorded or may have been exposed to minute quantities of DES residues in meat.

Genital disorders were also found in males, including epididymal cysts, irregular sperm, and microphallus.[66] The drug does not appear to be a carcinogen in DES sons, but often there is a latency period of twenty years or more between exposure and development of a tumor. Thus it is possible that both males and females might display high cancer rates sometime in the future.[67] However, because more than thirty years have passed since the initial exposures, with almost all exposures having occurred more than twenty years ago, the lack of significantly increased cancer in the DES mothers and their children (except for adenocarcinoma in DES daughters and a slight increase in cancer risk for DES mothers) can be interpreted as a good sign that future significant increases in cancer incidence are unlikely.

DES appears to produce teratogenic effects in nongenital organs. Like other estrogens, it is associated with cardiovascular irregularities, includ-

64. A. L. Herbst and others, "Age-Incidence and Risk of Diethylstilbestrol-Related Clear Cell Adenocarcinoma of the Vagina and Cervix," p. 43.

65. Herbst, "Written Testimony in the Matter of Diethylstilbestrol."

66. Bibbo, "Final Progress Report," pp. 12–18 and app. 3.

67. Ibid., p. 12.

ing transposition of the great arteries and valve defects. There also appears to be evidence of cleft palate.[68]

Finally, DES was discontinued as a preventive for miscarriages because it was found ineffective.[69]

Careful records concerning the doses of DES and related estrogens were kept for only a small number of women given the DES therapy.[70] Thus it is impossible to estimate either the dose or the actual incidence of adverse conditions. For children manifesting the effects, it was generally possible to learn whether DES or some other estrogen was administered to their mothers during pregnancy, but often it was impossible to estimate the dose. Thus the incidence of disorders and the estimates of dose are guesses. It is evident that doses were high, often in the range of 0.3 to 18.2 grams during pregnancy.[71]

There is some evidence of carcinogenicity of DES and other estrogens, as well as indications of cardiovascular problems. The pregnant women given DES appear to have a slight increase in cancer risk, particularly breast cancer;[72] in contrast, women treated with DES and other estrogens for other conditions appear to have a lower than normal risk of breast cancer.[73] Women treated with various estrogens following hysterectomy appear to have a higher risk of cancer; women treated for relief of menopausal symptoms, postmenopausal osteoporosis, or gonadal dysgenesis appear to have a higher risk of uterine cancers.[74] Men treated with DES

68. Olli P. Heinonen and others, "Cardiovascular Birth Defects and Antenatal Exposure to Female Sex Hormones," pp. 67–70; and FDA, "Initial Decision," p. 29.

69. Council for Agricultural Science and Technology, *Hormonally Active Substances in Foods: A Safety Evaluation*, p. 1.

70. Herbst, "Summary of the Changes in the Human Female Genital Tract as a Consequence of Maternal Diethylstilbestrol Therapy," pp. 14–15.

71. A. L. Herbst and others, "Clear-cell Adenocarcinoma of the Vagina and Cervix in Girls: Analysis of 1970 Registry Cases, p. 716; Olli P. Heinonen, "Diethylstilbestrol in Pregnancy: Frequency of Exposure and Usage Patterns," pp. 573–77; and Ann B. Barnes and others, "Fertility and Outcome of Pregnancy in Women Exposed in Utero to Diethylstilbestrol," p. 612.

72. John A. McLachlan and Robert L. Dixon, "Transplacental Toxicity of Diethylstilbestrol: A Special Problem in Safety Evaluation," pp. 432–33; Bibbo, "Final Progress Report," app. 4; and International Agency for Research on Cancer, *Monographs in Evaluation of Carcinogenic Risk*, vol. 6 (IARC, 1974).

73. George H. Gass, "A Discussion of Assay Sensitivity Methodology and Carcinogenic Potential," p. 114.

74. Bruce S. Cutler and others, "Endometrial Carcinoma after Stilbestrol Therapy in Gonadal Dysgenesis," pp. 628–730; A. M. McCarrol and others, "Endome-

for prostate cancer seem to have a slightly higher incidence of mammary tumors.[75] Men and women taking large doses of DES appear to have a higher incidence of atherosclerotic coronary vascular disease.[76] Oral contraceptives provide billions of person-years of experience of exposure to high doses of estrogen. There is no indication of increased carcinogenicity, although the oral contraceptives are teratogenic when taken after conception and are associated with some circulatory disease.[77] Thus DES appears to be similar to other estrogens in that it is a teratogen at high doses and is associated with cardiovascular disease. It also appears to be carcinogenic.

One early study found that DES daughters experienced some difficulty in becoming pregnant, although this result was not present in a larger, more complete study.[78] DES daughters, however, were found to have a significant increase in unfavorable pregnancy outcomes (relative risk 1.69 compared with controls) and higher proportions of miscarriages, ectopic pregnancies, stillbirths, premature births and failure to ever have a full-term live birth. The prevalence of several of these outcomes is associated with the higher dose of DES. Finally, there has been a suggestion that unfavorable outcomes to pregnancy are associated with structural defects of the cervix and vagina, although Barnes and associates did not

---

trial Carcinoma after Cyclical Oestrogen—Progestogen Therapy for Turner's Syndrome," pp. 421–23; and Noel S. Weiss, Daniel R. Szekely, and Donald F. Austin, "Increasing Incidence of Endometrial Cancer in the United States," pp. 1259–61.

75. IARC, *Monographs in Evaluation of Carcinogenic Risk;* H. H. Bulow and others, "Mamma-Carcinom bei oestrogenbehandeltem Prostata-Carcinom," pp. 249–53; and McLachlan and Dixon, "Transplacental Toxicity of Diethylstilbestrol," p. 432.

76. M. T. Morrell and S. C. Truelove, "Congestive Cardiac Failure Induced by Oestrogen Therapy," pp. 165–67; John C. Bailar III and David P. Byar, "Estrogen Treatment for Cancer of the Prostate: Early Results with 3 Doses of Diethylstilbestrol and Placebo," pp. 257–61; and McLachlan and Dixon, "Transplacental Toxicity of Diethylstilbestrol," p. 432.

77. Nicholas H. Booth, "Written Testimony in the Matter of Diethylstilbestrol: Withdrawal of Approval of New Animal Drug Applications," pp. 9–10. Actually, combined oral contraceptives appear to protect against endometrial and possibly breast cancer, while one sequential oral contraceptive (Oracon) is associated with a statistically significant increase in endometrial cancer. See Noel S. Weiss and Tom A. Sayvetz, "Incidence of Endometrial Cancer in Relation to the Use of Oral Contraceptives," pp. 551–54.

78. Marluce Bibbo and others, "Follow-up Study of Male and Female Offspring of DES-Exposed Mothers," pp. 1–8; and Barnes and others, "Fertility and Outcome of Pregnancy in Women Exposed in Utero to Diethylstilbestrol," pp. 610–11.

find such a relationship.[79] There is further suggestive evidence that DES sons have low fertility.[80]

DES has been subjected to a number of animal bioassay studies.[81] Animals display most of the effects found in humans and provide the advantage of study under controlled conditions. Bioassay studies using mice find genital cancer and mammary tumors in females and teratogenic effects in both females and males, including sterility and lower fertility.[82] Nongenital teratogenic effects include cardiovascular irregularities and cleft palate and lip.[83] In addition there is at least suggestive evidence that statistically significant effects occur for doses as low as 6.25 parts per billion, although the significance was not found in mice exposed to 12 and 25 ppb.[84] DES appears to be a mutagen in mice.[85]

Quantification of Risk

The lack of data on both dose and response for DES given to prevent miscarriage makes it impossible to estimate a dose-response relationship with confidence. Various risk estimates have been made, however, under the standard assumption of a no-threshold, linear dose-response relationship. For example, if all women in the United States consumed beef fattened with DES, their daughters would be expected to manifest an incidence of clear cell adenocarcinoma of from twelve cases every one hundred

79. Barnes and others, "Fertility and Outcome of Pregnancy in Women Exposed in Utero to Diethylstilbestrol," p. 613.

80. W. B. Gill, Gebhard F. B. Schumacher, and Marluce Bibbo, "Structural and Functional Abnormalities in Sex Organs of Male Offspring of Mothers Treated with Diethylstilbestrol (DES)," pp. 147–53; and A. E. Stenchever, "Possible Relationship of Males Exposed to DES and Sexual Abnormalities," Reproductive Genetics Laboratory, University of Washington (n.d.).

81. For example, see McLachlan and Dixon, "Transplacental Toxicity of Diethylstilbestrol," pp. 435–41; and Gass, Coats, and Graham, "Carcinogenic Dose-Response Curve to Oral Diethylstilbestrol," pp. 971–77.

82. McLachlan and Dixon, "Transplacental Toxicity of Diethylstilbestrol," pp. 435–41.

83. Gass, "A Discussion of Assay Sensitivity Methodology and Carcinogenic Potential."

84. Gass, Coats, and Graham, "Carcinogenic Dose-Response Curve to Oral Diethylstilbestrol," p. 976.

85. C. Larry Chrisman, "Aneuploidy in Mouse Embryos Induced by Diethylstilbestrol Diphosphate"; and C. L. Chrisman and L. L. Hinkel, "Induction of Aneuploidy in Mouse Bone Marrow Cells with Diethylstilbestrol Diphosphate," pp. 831–35.

years to essentially zero.[86] Teratogenic risks can be estimated based on the assumption that 50 percent of the fetuses exposed to DES as a drug to prevent miscarriage (a dose of 1.07–64.0 milligrams a day) had serious malformations. DES in beef would lead to an exposure of about 1.9 nanograms a day. Assuming a linear, no-threshold dose-response relationship between malformations and DES exposure, one would expect 2.6 malformations among the 3 million babies born each year. In view of the conservative assumptions behind this calculation, it is more likely that there would be far fewer than one malformation each year due to DES in beef.[87]

As noted earlier, there is little evidence that DES causes mammary tumors in women, but it does in mice and appears to in men.[88] One might attempt to extrapolate this risk to humans. Using the double extrapolation of going from mice to humans and from high to low doses, one can estimate the effect of consuming beef liver containing 2 ppb of DES and muscle meat containing 0.2 ppb. Using data from Gass and associates, the

86. Thomas H. Jukes ("Testimony in the Matter of Diethylstilbestrol: Withdrawal of Approval of New Animal Drug Applications," p. 11) estimates that there is not more than one clear cell carcinoma every 133 to 3,800 years in the U.S. population. Jones and Grendon ("Environmental Factors in the Origin of Cancer and Estimation of the Possible Hazards to Man") estimate the risk per year to be 0.12 to 1×10^{-7}. See also Booth, "Written Testimony in the Matter of Diethylstilbestrol"; and OTA, *Drugs in Livestock Feed*, vol. 1, pp. 53–55. The dose is assumed to be 0.2 ppb in liver and 0.02 ppb in muscle meat, or lower. But even a dose ten times higher would produce a negligible effect.

87. The estimate assumes consumption of 0.7 kilogram of liver a year containing 0.12 ppb and 52 kilograms of muscle containing 0.012 ppb of DES. Thus annual consumption of DES would be 708 nanograms, or 1.9 ng a day (see Jukes, "Testimony in the Matter of Diethystilbestrol," p. 9). According to Heinonen ("Diethylstilbestrol in Pregnancy," p. 575), the median dose prescribed for pregnant women was 84 milligrams a day. If half of the children who received 84 milligrams of DES a day had congenital malformations, and if the dose-response curve were linear-no threshold, this would mean that the current risk from beef consumption is 1.1×10^{-8}. Assuming that 3 million babies are born each year, one could expect 0.033 malformations a year. As an alternative calculation, one could assume that all the beef liver contains 2 ppb and muscle contains 0.2 ppb. If so, the risk would be 17.4 times greater and thus 0.58 malformations would be expected each year.

DES residues are not uniformly distributed across carcasses; if the effect is nonlinear, there is the possibility that a particular liver, which contains several times the acceptable level, might exert a larger than expected effect. If the effect is nonlinear, however, the estimates above almost certainly overstate the expected effects of DES. Thus, if anything, the ill effects of DES would be lower than estimated.

88. McLachlan and Dixon, "Transplacental Toxicity of Diethylstilbestrol," pp. 435–41; and Gass, Coats, and Graham, "Carcinogenic Dose-Response Curve to Oral Diethylstilbestrol."

Office of Technology Assessment (OTA) estimated human risks of mammary tumors to be 1 in 13,000 (per lifetime) based on female mice and 1 in 82,000 (per lifetime) based on male mice.[89] Assuming these estimates hold for 111 million females and 105 million males, one would expect DES to cause 8,538 breast cancers in women and 1,280 breast cancers in men over their lifetimes. This implies an annual incidence rate of approximately 110 breast cancers in women and 18 breast cancers in men. The estimated current annual incidence of breast cancers is 110,000 for women and 900 for men.[90] Thus the OTA estimates make DES responsible for 0.1 percent of the observed breast cancers in women and 2.2 percent of the observed breast cancers in men. DES is estimated to be responsible for such a tiny increase in the incidence of breast cancer that the change could not be detected empirically. Minor changes in the extrapolation procedure could reduce these estimates to zero or raise them somewhat. According to Jukes, DES concentration in meat is 18.6 times lower than that assumed by OTA; if so, the annual incidence of breast cancer due to DES would be six for women and one for men.[91]

The Net Effect of Using DES for Cattle Growth

The presence of estrogens in the blood of cattle increases the efficiency with which feed is digested and metabolized.[92] Thus bulls gain weight more quickly and with less feed per pound of extra weight than do steers in feedlots. Bulls, however, are more difficult to handle, and the meat is deemed to have a less desirable flavor. DES is a synthetic, inexpensive hormone that produces the weight gain of natural estrogens in steers without the behavioral effect or flavor change. The DES is utilized either as an implant in the ear (which gradually releases the drug over 120 days before slaughter) or as a direct supplement to the feed.[93] Various studies show that DES decreases the feed required to fatten steers by 7–12 percent and speeds weight gain 15–19 percent; evidence also shows that DES acts to

89. OTA, *Drugs in Livestock Feed*, p. 55.
90. Incidence estimates are based on rates from the National Cancer Institute SER program, 1973–77, contained in American Cancer Society, *Cancer: Facts and Figures for 1981* (ACS, 1981).
91. Jukes, "Testimony in the Matter of Diethylstilbestrol."
92. OTA, *Drugs in Livestock Feed*, pp. 36–38; and Thomas H. Jukes, "Diethylstilbestrol in Beef Production: What Is the Risk?"
93. CAST, *Hormonally Active Substances in Foods*, p. 8.

increase slightly the ratio of lean meat to fat.[94] Headley's estimates imply that the prohibition of DES (without substituting another weight-gain drug) would increase beef prices 9.1 percent the first year, thus costing Americans about $5 billion in the first year because of the need for additional grain and handling of animals; FDA estimates the cost to be $523 million a year.[95]

Adding DES to the diets of steers has two undesired consequences. The first is that the high doses of DES often cause abscesses in the steer's liver, making it unsuitable for sale.[96] When this occurs, the carcass is worth about $2.50 to $5 less. The second is that the estrogen tends to promote sexual activity in steers.[97] In hot weather and crowded pens, this activity takes the form of some steers mounting others, causing damage to the steer mounted (buller). The damage is estimated to amount to approximately $25–$60 per buller. Between 1 and 4 percent of steers are bullers and suffer this damage.[98] Thus the efficiency in weight gain is partially offset by the cost of buying and administering the DES, the liver damage, and the bullers. It is evident, however, that DES still offers a net benefit to feedlots.

Since DES increases the speed with which steers gain weight and lowers the amount of grain needed to fatten them, the cost to consumers of banning DES is estimated to be $0.5–5 billion during the first year. Clearly DES is worth a great deal,[99] but in large doses it is a teratogen and appears

94. M. L. Ogilvie and others, "Effects of Stilbestrol in Altering Carcass Composition and Feed Lot Performance of Beef Steers," pp. 991–1001. Also see review in Jukes, "Testimony in the Matter of Diethylstilbestrol," pp. 15–16; and OTA, *Drugs in Livestock Feed,* pp. 37–38. Ogilvie and associates find DES increases protein 1.7 to 4.8 percent, decreases fat 4.2 percent to 16.7 percent, and increases moisture 1.1 to 3.8 percent. The largest effects occur in animals fed DES the shortest time (56 days) and least effects occur in animals fed the longest time (168 days).

95. J. C. Headley ("Economic Aspects of Drug and Chemical Feed Additives," p. 22) estimates that banning DES would cause beef prices to rise 9.1 percent during the first year of a ban (and less through year seven, then more). Beef consumption is about 126 pounds per person per year. Assume that beef sells at retail for about $2 a pound. Then 27.24 billion pounds of beef are consumed, selling for $54.47 billion each year. A 9.1 percent increase in price would cost an additional $5 billion during the first year. FDA, "Initial Decision," p. 20.

96. FDA, "Initial Decision," p. 21.

97. R. E. Pierson and others, "Bulling among Yearling Feedlot Steers," *Journal of the American Veterinary Medical Association,* vol. 169 (September 1976), pp. 521–23.

98. Ibid.

99. A number of drugs, including natural hormones, however, also speed weight gain. See OTA, *Drugs in Livestock Feed.*

to be a carcinogen. Neither these effects nor the extrapolated estimate of mammary tumors (from those found in rats) appear to pose a perceptible risk to humans when the DES is present in beef at minimum detectable levels or below. Although there is an extremely small theoretical risk of harm to humans from the presence of small amounts of DES in beef, the effects could not be identified among natural occurrences of disease. If DES acts like natural estrogens, this risk appears even smaller.[100] All humans have levels of estrogens in their bodies that are high relative to the level that might result from eating beef containing DES.[101] In addition grains, vegetables, and meat from animals that were not given DES all contain hormonally active substances.[102] The dose of hormone-active substances from these other sources also appears large relative to that of DES from beef.[103] The body regulates the production of natural estrogens by monitoring hormone levels in the blood. Presumably an increase in blood hormones due to ingesting DES, animal hormones, or hormone-active substances would lead to decreased production of hormones and maintenance of normal levels with no carcinogenic or teratogenic effects. Only if DES effects were different from natural substances would there be reason for concern.

Finally, feeding steers DES need not lead to levels nearly as large as 2 ppb in the steers' livers. Levels this high result from failing to observe the statutory withdrawal time of fourteen days, inadvertently feeding cattle grain contaminated with DES, or some similar mistake.[104] The Department of Agriculture sampling program has found that only between 0.8 and 1.7 percent of the steer livers tested in 1977 contained measurable (more than 0.5 ppb) of DES.[105] This may be an underestimate, however,

100. Kliman, "Testimony in the Matter of Diethylstilbestrol," pp. 6–9; and Elwood V. Jensen, "Written Direct Testimony in the Matter of Diethylstilbestrol: Withdrawal of Approval of New Animal Drug Applications," pp. 5–6.

101. CAST, *Hormonally Active Substances in Foods*, p. 5; Kliman, "Testimony in the Matter of Diethylstilbestrol," pp. 7–10; and John A. McLachlan, "Written Testimony in the Matter of Diethylstilbestrol," pp. 5–6. The latter presents the theory that DES and endogenous estrogens behave in different ways.

102. CAST, *Hormonally Active Substances in Foods*, p. 17.

103. See review in ibid., pp. 17–21.

104. T. S. Rumsey and others ("Depletion Patterns of Radioactivity and Tissue Residues in Beef Cattle after Withdrawal of Oral ^{14}C-Diethylstilbestrol," pp. 539–49) discuss the time required to metabolize or eliminate DES. Also see Philip Sheeler, "Testimony in the Matter of Diethylstilbestrol: Withdrawal of Approval of New Animal Drug Applications."

105. Bert Levy, "Testimony in the Matter of Diethylstilbestrol: Withdrawal of Approval of New Animal Drug Applications."

because of testing procedures. Rather than banning DES, one might simply enforce withdrawal times to ensure that all steer livers contain less than 0.5 ppb. For example, the seller of an animal could be fined several thousand dollars for every animal found to have more than 0.5 ppb in its liver. Since this fine would be large relative to the savings from using DES, those feedlots that could not maintain withdrawal times would not use DES.

The cost of banning DES could be smaller than the estimated $0.5 billion to $5 billion a year. Other supplements could replace DES at nearly the same cost and give similar effects on weight gain efficiency.[106] Each substitute has problems, however. Other estrogens would have effects similar to DES in respect to both weight gain and carcinogenicity and teratogenicity.[107] They would have two advantages over DES. The first is that they would have less of an emotional overtone, since they are not identified by the public as responsible for hundreds of cancers and hundreds of thousands of malformations. If DES now has an emotional association like that of thalidomide, there may be no alternative to substituting some other drug. The second advantage is that they are natural hormones. Insofar as DES arouses significant suspicion because it is synthetic, substituting natural hormones would allay fears.

Subtherapeutic doses of antibiotics are currently used to speed growth and weight gain and could serve as a partial substitute for DES, but this practice is inherently suspicious since the low doses of antibiotics present an environment ideal for mutating bacteria into antibiotic resistant strains, as happened for one strain of gonorrhea.[108] The potential effects on human health are catastrophic, although it is virtually impossible to estimate when the effects might occur and how much morbidity and mortality might be produced.

Feedlot operators and packers have testified against banning DES, but the availability of substitutes and the emotion associated with the drug tended to mute this opposition. Nonetheless, the health effects of other estrogens are probably no lower and those of subtherapeutic doses of antibiotics are probably much greater. To prevent worse consequences, the FDA should have considered the entire group of growth stimulants before banning DES. Since the ban on DES, the Department of Agricul-

106. In OTA, *Drugs in Livestock Feed*, pp. 29–36, there is a review of substitutes for DES.
107. Ibid., pp. 36–37.
108. Ibid., pp. 29–36, 41–45.

ture has reported widespread violation of the ban.[109] Thus one can infer that feedlot operators find the ban so costly that they are willing to go to some lengths and take risks to obtain the drug.

Aflatoxin

Aflatoxin is the product of a mold that grows on grain and nuts.[110] It is found to be a potent carcinogen in rats and other animals, and there is suggestive evidence that it is a liver carcinogen in humans.[111] Aflatoxin is a contaminant of foods, not an additive. Thus it is difficult to lower the concentration of aflatoxins in some foods and impossible to eliminate it. The current tolerance level is 20 ppb and the FDA has proposed lowering this level to 15 ppb.[112] Since aflatoxin has no beneficial effects, is known to be an animal carcinogen, and is likely to be a human carcinogen, it is evident that concentrations should be low. Tempering this desire is the difficulty and expense of lowering concentrations. Thus the question for regulators is how low the tolerance level ought to be.

The Risks of Aflatoxin in Food

The molds *Aspergillus flavus* and *Aspergillus parasiticus* grow on grains and nuts under warm, moist conditions. Ordinarily the grain and nut kernels are protected by a covering, but when the covering is mechanically damaged, as by insects or other molds and bacteria, *A. flavus* spores can more easily gain entrance to the grain and germinate. Aflatoxin concentrations are higher in the southeastern United States than in other U.S.

109. "Ante-Mortem Inspection: DES in Cattle-Certification of Reconditioning," *Federal Register,* vol. 45 (April 22, 1980), pp. 26947–50.

110. NAS, *Food Safety Policy,* pp. 3-45 to 3-48; Gerald N. Wogan, "Mycotoxins and Other Naturally Occurring Carcinogens," p. 265; and Ronald C. Shank, "Epidemiology of Aflatoxin Carcinogenesis," p. 292.

111. See review in U.S. Food and Drug Administration, "Assessment of Estimated Risk Resulting from Aflatoxins in Consumer Peanut Products and Other Food Commodities," pp. 1, 10–17. See also F. G. Peers and C. A. Linsell, "Dietary Aflatoxins and Liver Cancer: A Population Based Study in Kenya," pp. 473–83; S. J. van Rensburg, "Role of Epidemiology in Elucidation of Mycotoxin Health Risks," pp. 705–10; S. J. van Rensburg and others, "Primary Liver Cancer and Aflatoxin in a High Cancer Area," pp. 2508a–08d; and Wogan, "Mycotoxins and Other Naturally Occurring Carcinogens," pp. 266–72.

112. FDA, "Assessment of Estimated Risk Resulting from Aflatoxins," p. 1.

regions.[113] Concentrations are even higher in some African countries (Uganda, Kenya, Mozambique, and Swaziland) and in Thailand.[114] The toxin can be transmitted to meat, eggs, and milk through animals being fed contaminated grain.[115]

Aflatoxin is a potent liver carcinogen in rats. Moreover, in a suggestive epidemiological study the aflatoxin levels in grains in the five countries mentioned above were measured and compared with the incidence of liver cancer in those countries. Although a significant positive relationship suggests that aflatoxin is a potent carcinogen in humans, it appears that this study failed to control for other factors (for example, hepatitis), which may have been involved causally in much of the observed cancer.[116]

People in the southeastern United States are estimated to consume an average of 2.7 (with a maximum of 9.0) nanograms of aflatoxin per kilogram of body weight per day.[117] Since people in other regions eat less corn, and since the grains they eat contain less aflatoxin, they probably consume a small fraction of this amount, perhaps only 10 percent as much. Thus other factors held constant, one would expect a much higher rate of liver cancer in the Southeast than in other regions. Actually, the reverse obtains, presumably because of factors other than aflatoxin exposures.

When the linear dose-response relationship estimated for Mozambique and Asia is applied to aflatoxin doses experienced in the American Southeast (based on rates in Georgia and Alabama) liver cancer is estimated to account for 20.2 to 67 of each 100,000 deaths. Since liver cancer results in about 100 of each 100,000 deaths in the Southeast, aflatoxin is estimated to account for between 20 and 67 percent of liver cancers there. Could aflatoxin account for much or even most of the liver cancer in the Southeast, where it is most concentrated, but little or none of the higher (161 per 100,000 deaths) incidence of liver cancer throughout the rest of the United States? The epidemiological results do not appear to be a valid indicator of the risks to Americans of aflatoxin.

Aflatoxin is a potent carcinogen in rats and in other animals, but is

113. Ibid.
114. Shank, "Epidemiology of Aflatoxin Carcinogenesis," pp. 293–315.
115. FDA, "Assessment of Estimated Risk Resulting from Aflatoxins," p. 1; and Council for Agricultural Science and Technology, *Aflatoxin and Other Mycotoxins: An Agricultural Perspective*, p. 1.
116. Information in this paragraph is from FDA, "Assessment of Estimated Risk Resulting from Aflatoxins," pp. 3, 15; and Shank, "Epidemiology of Aflatoxin Carcinogenesis," pp. 307, 315.
117. FDA, "Assessment of Estimated Risk Resulting from Aflatoxins," p. 2.

much less potent in mice.[118] Extrapolating from rats to humans and to somewhat lower doses, one would expect to find aflatoxin in the Southeast caused 240 to 1,100 liver cancers per 100,000 deaths, which is 140 percent to 1,000 percent too high. Extrapolating from all animals would lead to an estimated incidence in the Southeast of 17 to 126 liver cancers for each 100,000 deaths. This estimate is closer to the results of the epidemiological study than those for rats.

While there are problems with the studies, one might use these epidemiological data to estimate the number of liver cancers caused by aflatoxin. I assume that 10 percent of Americans are exposed to high aflatoxin levels and the other 90 percent are exposed to levels only 10 percent this high. Then 22 million people would have a liver cancer rate of 1.8–6.0 per million people per year and 198 million people would have a liver cancer rate of 0.18–0.60 per million per year. Thus 75–251 people would be estimated to get liver cancer each year from aflatoxin. If exposure to aflatoxin were reduced 50 percent, 38–126 people would be saved each year.

Eliminating Aflatoxin from Foods

Aflatoxin is not uniformly distributed; it is concentrated in some grains, but the vast majority of grains have none. Although virtually all contaminated peanuts can be eliminated by mechanical sorting, there is no current system for mechanically sorting corn and other grains.

The mold could be inhibited by planting more resistant strains (presumably), by lowering insect damage, by harvesting the crops early (before there is time for the mold to grow), by better handling and dry storage conditions, by using fungicides, or by such radical techniques as prohibiting peanuts as human food and not growing corn in the Southeast. More intense use of pesticides would probably lower insect damage, although it would leave larger residues of pesticides in the food. Earlier harvesting would often necessitate mechanical drying. Fungicides would kill the mold. All these proposals are costly, and using pesticides and fungicides more intensely would bring some increased health risk to the consumer from any residual, while greater energy use would increase occupational and consumer risks.

No estimates have been made of the cost of reducing aflatoxin. If the

118. NAS, *Food Safety Policy,* pp. 3–53.

FDA set a lower tolerance level of aflatoxin in food, this would stimulate investigation of the ways of reducing the growth of the mold or of sorting out contaminated kernels. But first a crude benefit-cost analysis should be done to decide whether the benefits of lowering the tolerance level are likely to exceed the costs.

Saccharin

Perhaps the most controversial food additive has been saccharin. This nonnutritive sweetener was discovered almost a century ago but has been suspected throughout most of this period of being a toxin. A vast literature documents animal bioassays testing the carcinogenicity of saccharin and the impurities that occur in its manufacture. The early results were often contradictory. Furthermore, the animal bioassays raised questions about whether one could extrapolate to humans and whether the very high doses received by the animals overwhelmed their immune system or otherwise led to an abnormal metabolic uptake.

If saccharin were a carcinogen, but one of very low potency, the seemingly contradictory results of the animal bioassays would be explicable. But if it exhibited such low potency in laboratory rats, there would have to be doubts about whether it was a carcinogen in humans. One series of epidemiological studies has focused on persons receiving high doses, such as diabetics.[119] Although no elevation in cancer rates was found, the results are particularly difficult to interpret since the diabetes or other unusual characteristics might protect the individuals against cancer in some way, leading to a spurious finding of little or no effect. Three recent epidemiological studies have been reported, all of which failed to find significant increases in bladder cancer related to saccharin use.[120] The largest study found an increase among the heaviest users, particularly among

119. Bruce Armstrong and others, "Cancer Mortality and Saccharin Consumption in Diabetics," pp. 151–57; and Irving I. Kessler, "Cancer Mortality Among Diabetics," pp. 673–86.

120. Alan S. Morrison and Julie E. Buring, "Artifical Sweeteners and Cancer of the Lower Urinary Tract," pp. 537–41; Robert Hoover and others, "Progress Report to the Food and Drug Administration from the National Cancer Institute Concerning the National Bladder Cancer Study"; and Ernst L. Wynder and Steven D. Stellman, "Artificial Sweetener Use and Bladder Cancer: A Case Control Study," pp. 1214–16.

heavy smokers.[121] For a carcinogen of very low potency, it is almost impossible to construct an epidemiological study whose conclusions one can have confidence in.

The epidemiological results might be interpreted in one of three ways: (1) saccharin is a carcinogen of low potency that is causing a small increase in bladder cancer, (2) saccharin is not a human carcinogen, and (3) a long enough latency period is involved for a significant elevation of bladder cancer rates to occur in the future.[122] The best interpretation of current evidence, however, is that saccharin is not a human carcinogen or that it produces effects too small to be measurable.

As a food additive, saccharin is governed by the general FDA statute against introducing noxious substances into food and in particular by the Delaney Clause. The FDA decided there was sufficient evidence of carcinogenicity and banned saccharin, giving rise to considerable controversy. It is important to realize that for most food additives there are many substitute compounds, and little cost is involved in banning the use of one. (Thus FDA spokesmen defend the Delaney Clause and the vast majority of food additive decisions.) Saccharin, however, is an unusual case in that cyclamate, the only other nonnutritive sweetener licensed, was banned in 1969 as a carcinogen. The banning of saccharin therefore threatened to leave an increasingly disaffected public without any nonnutritive sweetener.

If banning a suspected carcinogen results in little or no loss to the public, then the only issue the FDA should consider is how much evidence of carcinogenicity is necessary to justify banning a compound. Obviously, the greater the cost to the public, the more conclusive the evidence should be.

When an additive has no close substitutes, the FDA studies what effect its removal from use would have on the quality and availability of food. Sassafras tea was banned because it contains the carcinogen safarole and was not considered an important food by the FDA. In banning saccharin, the FDA rejected the argument that it is important to offer the public a nonnutritive sweetener.

Running through this controversy is a profound disagreement about values. Some contend that no one needs saccharin and that people who

121. Hoover and others, "Progress Report," pp. 26–27.
122. Morrison and Buring, "Artificial Sweeteners and Cancer of the Lower Urinary Tract," p. 541.

desire it should be ignored, even if they are willing to pay a great deal for it and to organize political pressure.[123] Saccharin users, in other words, are behaving like children eating too much candy; the FDA has an obligation to take away the candy to protect them. Others believe that adults are the best judge of what they themselves should consume, as long as they are reasonably well informed about the dangers.[124] If adults are considered to be responsible for themselves and their children, and if they can exercise choice on the basis of reasonable information, then the Delaney Clause can be justified only as a device to save the public the cost of discovering information about a substance it costs nothing to ban. If people do not have a choice (because of the range of additives in processed food), cannot acquire or understand the information, or prefer not to make this decision, then the FDA should act to protect them. These questions and differences in attitude are so basic that resolution is essentially impossible. Regulation of saccharin and other food additives is likely to proceed on an ad hoc basis; perhaps general principles will emerge from the individual cases, although agreement on the philosophical principles seems unlikely.

A Summary of Present Regulation

The FDA has determined there is insufficient evidence to show sodium nitrite to be a carcinogen.[125] It has withdrawn its proposal to limit the use of sodium nitrite to cured meats to protect against botulism only; to ban amounts greater than those required for botulism protection; and to phase out use (an action contingent on finding an acceptable substitute, although the timing was designed to force industry to search for an acceptable alternative). Nitrosamines are carcinogens, and the FDA could take the position that consuming nitrite inevitably meant consuming nitrosamines. Instead, the agency is attempting to eliminate preformed nitrosamines without concern for those resulting from ingesting nitrite. Since a concern with only preformed nitrosamines makes little sense, one might conclude that the FDA seemed to be searching for a rationale to back off from a proposed ban.

123. Dan E. Beauchamp, "Public Health and Individual Liberty," pp. 121–36.
124. Milton Friedman, *Capitalism and Freedom.*
125. U.S. Food and Drug Administration, press release, August 19, 1980.

The FDA has determined that DES is a carcinogen and has banned its use as a growth stimulant for beef and other meat-producing animals.[126]

Because aflatoxin is not a food additive it is not covered by the Delaney Clause. Nonetheless, the FDA, under its interpretation of the Federal Food, Drug and Cosmetic Act (section 406 concerning poisonous and deleterious substances), has set a tolerance level of 20 ppb based on ability to detect.[127] The FDA has proposed lowering the tolerance level to 15 ppb in response to improvements in detection technology.[128] Since aflatoxin can be detected at a few ppb, the standard could be made much more stringent.

Saccharin was considered by the FDA in a full, formal process and then banned. Before the ban became effective, however, Congress forbade the FDA to enforce it for eighteen months in order to get additional evidence. That respite expired in May 1979 and has since been renewed, although there is no new contradiction to the carcinogenicity of saccharin in animal bioassays.

Applications of the Eight Frameworks

Table 1 summarizes the regulatory actions that would be implied by the application of each of the decision frameworks to four additives or contaminants (in addition to current FDA regulations). Needless to say this table is highly tentative at best and incomplete because of the inability to survey the range of programs as required for the cost-effectiveness and regulatory budget frameworks.

Market Regulation

If producers and consumers were left to their own decisions, the FDA's role would be limited to ensuring that products were correctly labeled. Part of the label might be reserved for toxic materials and their concentrations in the food.

126. U.S. Food and Drug Administration, "Initial Decision for Docket No. 76N-0002 by Administrative Law Judge Daniel J. Davidson" (September 21, 1978).
127. Merrill, "Federal Regulation of Cancer-Causing Chemicals," chap. 2, p. 51.
128. Ibid., p. 52.

Table 1. Application of Decision Frameworks to Additives and Contaminants

Decision framework	Implied regulatory action for:			
	Nitrite	DES	Aflatoxin	Saccharin
Market regu-lation	No action	No action	No action	No action
No risk	Ban	Ban	Levels as low as technologi-cally feasible	Ban
Technology-based standards	Ban	Ban	Levels as low as technologi-cally feasible	Ban
Risk-risk	Low amounts permitted	No action	No action	Ban
Risk versus benefits	No excess permitted	Careful use permitted	Fairly stringent	No action
Cost-effec-tiveness	No agency attention	No agency attention	More attention and control	No agency attention
Regulatory budget	No agency attention	No agency attention	More attention and control	No agency attention
Benefit-cost	No excess permitted	Careful use permitted	More stringent than present	No action

DES = Diethylstilbestrol.

No-Risk

Sodium nitrite, DES, and saccharin pose risks to consumers; all would be banned under a no-risk framework. Aflatoxin also poses risks to consumers; while it cannot be banned, steps could be taken to lower exposure by banning the use of peanuts as a food and by forbidding the production of corn in the Southeast. Obviously the FDA is reluctant to adopt a strict no-risk criterion; of the four substances, only DES is banned. Congress took action on saccharin and threatened action on nitrite.

Technology-Based Regulation

Best available technology is easy to apply to additives; they can simply be banned. The concept is unclear for a contaminant since there are many ways of lowering exposure, including banning peanut products and the growing of corn in the Southeast. Technology exists to lower aflatoxin in peanut butter below 15 ppb. Thus the FDA's current regulation is not even one reflecting best available control technology.

Risk-Risk

The indirect risk-risk framework could not be implemented within this study since an extensive analysis is required to identify the health and safety effects per unit of output for each industry and then to use the input-output framework. Safety data are readily available, but there are less data on disease effects. Nonetheless, implementing this framework is more a matter of hard work than of creativity.

The direct risk-risk framework is not applicable to DES or aflatoxin, since neither when present in food conveys any health benefits to consumers. Presumably saccharin offers health benefits in the form of reduced weight due to lower caloric intake, more frequent brushing of teeth because of saccharin-sweetened toothpaste, and better social adjustment for diabetics through having beverages that can be consumed socially. None of these benefits have been quantified satisfactorily, however, and one can only conjecture about their magnitude and importance.[129]

In order to use this framework for sodium nitrite, the incidence of botulism and resulting mortality must be estimated for several concentrations of nitrite in cured meat, and especially for banning nitrite from cured meat. Since nitrite effectively inhibits *C. botulinum,* cured meat is treated casually now. If that continued and if meat processing were continued as at present, botulism could become a common disease. Present experience indicates that about 25 percent of people with botulism die. Conceivably, banning nitrite could lead to a great many deaths each year.

But it is nonsense to believe that habits would remain unchanged if nitrite were banned.[130] It is likely that cured meats would be shipped, sold, and stored in a frozen state.[131] A massive education campaign would be needed to teach consumers not to leave cured meats unrefrigerated and not to eat meats that had been unrefrigerated for more than a day. Botulism would result only when the delivery system failed or consumers acted stupidly out of ignorance or absentmindedness. How often would it happen that the refrigeration system of a delivery truck or meat locker would break down for several days without the results being reported? How often

129. National Academy of Sciences, *Saccharin: Technical Assessment of Risks and Benefits,* pp. 4-1 through 4-52; and Robert Hoover, "Saccharin—Bitter Aftertaste," pp. 573–74.

130. FDA and USDA, "FDA's and USDA's Action Regarding Nitrite," p. 44.

131. Frozen meat would be more difficult to handle because inadvertent thawing would permit bacteria to grow.

would consumers eat cured meat that had been in the refrigerator for more than a week or that had been unrefrigerated for several days? A close inspection of such meat might not reveal signs of spoilage, but the meat could still contain deadly levels of the toxin. The risks are especially large for the elderly and the poor who keep food in the refrigerator longer and who may have their electricity turned off.

Green has attempted to estimate the inestimable by examining the incidence of botulism in France due to cured meats that do not contain nitrite.[132] She then assumed that the rate of contamination per pound of meat in France could be extrapolated for application to the United States. This assumption led to estimates of nine deaths from contaminated ham, four from luncheon meats, and five from bacon each year. These estimates are crude and cannot be taken to be more than the roughest indications of what might be observed in practice, but there is at least a rough basis for the estimate that about eighteen deaths from botulism a year would result from banning nitrite.

Green estimated that about eight deaths a year would result from the nitrosopyrrolidine in bacon. Her estimates suggest that the health benefits of adding nitrite to cured meats are about equal to the health costs, or somewhat greater. Thus the risk-risk framework would suggest that nitrite should not be banned until a substitute is found that would confer the same protection against botulism but have lower cancer risk.

While the indirect risk-risk framework cannot be implemented, one can infer how it might modify the previous conclusions. By looking more widely at the health effects of a regulation that results in more man-hours per unit of output, the effect would be to increase the estimated health costs of the regulation. Thus this framework would bolster the conclusion that sodium nitrite should not be banned immediately from cured meats. Banning DES would have no observable effect on consumer health but would require more grain and feedlots; this framework would estimate the additional occupational injuries and disease for farmers, grain haulers, feedlot operators, and those making tractors and other capital goods. It would also suggest a reason for not banning DES. Doing so would raise by 7–12 percent the amount of feed required to fatten steers and would lengthen the time spent in the feedlot. Raising the additional grain and running the additional feedlots would result in some increase in occupational injuries and disease. As a partial offset, lower occupational expo-

132. Laura Green, "A Risk/Risk Analysis for Nitrite," pp. 13–20.

sure to DES would lower the incidence of some symptoms. By considering health effects more generally, this framework would begin to offer at least an offset to the cancers and malformations estimated to result from DES. Without more specific information on occupational disease and accidents, one cannot be confident they are greater than consumer risks, although this seems likely. The framework offers reasons for not regulating aflatoxin down to as low a level as feasible. Such a regulation would result in increased pesticide and fungicide use, more mechanical drying, more sorting, and additional grain production, all of which would increase occupational health costs to some degree. These costs, in going from 20 to 15 ppb, are unlikely to outweigh the benefits to consumers, but at some level of control further tightening would cost more in occupational diseases and injuries than would be saved consumers. Banning saccharin would have little effect on the production of saccharin substitutes. A small amount of additional sugar might be consumed, but the effect would most likely be small unless one thinks that Americans would not adjust their calorie consumption downward.

General Balancing of Risks Against Benefits

This framework, and its more rigorous analogue in benefit-cost analysis, allows consideration of nonhealth consequences of regulation. These come primarily in the form of increased cost and a less attractive product, as judged by consumers.

Banning sodium nitrite would require a large increase in refrigeration capacity at the processing facilities, in transportation, in markets, and in homes.[133] This increased storage means increased energy use, more capital goods, and more repairmen. In addition, more cured meat would be condemned because of commercial refrigeration breakdowns. Without nitrite, the taste and color of cured meats would be less appealing.

Thus this framework would further tip the scales against banning nitrite because of the additional costs of refrigeration and spoilage and the loss of cured meat products. When these considerations are added to the health risks, it is evident that banning nitrite would be so costly that it should not be done until substitutes are found to protect against botulism and to preserve the attractiveness of cured meats.

DES is largely a trade-off between the risk of cancer or malformation

133. FDA and USDA, "FDA's and USDA's Action Regarding Nitrite," pp. 42–44.

and the lower price of beef. Risk-benefit is the first framework appropriate for considering DES; the earlier frameworks are so narrow as to be inadequate. The occupational health effects of raising more feedgrains and running more feedlots are only a small part of the cost of banning DES. The total costs of the extra grain and extra feedlots must be weighed against the additional risk of cancer and malformation. The former effects consist of accidents, chronic disease, pollution, and greater land use; they involve costs measured in the billions of dollars each year. The latter risk involves fewer than 100 people a year, save for possible mutagenic effects that are unquantified. This framework probably would not lead to a banning of DES.

The costs of lowering exposure to aflatoxin include the cost of the additional grain, fungicides, dry storage, sorting, handling and processing, chemical analyses, earlier harvesting, mechanical drying, and developing more resistant grains.[134] This framework would lead to a higher tolerance level of aflatoxin in food than the earlier frameworks, since additional costs are being counted against regulation and the benefits of the regulation are not estimated to rise.

The primary reason for consuming saccharin is the pleasure derived from a nonnutritive sweetener; possible health benefits are a small part of the reason for consumption. With the exception of children, consumers would seem to be capable of weighing the small risk of cancer against their perceived benefit. Both risks and benefits accrue to the same individual. Consumers have been warned of the carcinogenicity of saccharin; either they must be deemed incapable of making a judgment or their decisions must be accepted.

Regulatory Budget and Cost-Effectiveness

The essence of both the cost-effectiveness and regulatory budget frameworks is the comparison among alternative actions an agency might take that would enhance health. This study has not considered the general nature of actions the FDA might take to enhance food safety, although one can conjecture that more lives could be saved by focusing on biological and chemical contamination than on food additives. Among the four substances considered here, the one with the greatest implication for health is probably aflatoxin contamination. DES involves very few lives and requires expenditures of billions of dollars a year for additional feed

134. CAST, *Aflatoxin and Other Mycotoxins*, pp. 17–22.

and feedlots; banning nitrite would not save lives (since botulism deaths would probably exceed the decrease in cancer deaths) and would increase expenditures and involve billions of dollars of losses in consumer surplus.[135] Banning saccharin would involve few lives and a large loss in consumer satisfaction; thus probably aflatoxin would be the focus of attention among these four substances under either a cost-effectiveness or a regulatory budget framework. It seems unlikely, however, that even aflatoxin would receive much attention, given the other opportunities open to the FDA to control biological and chemical contamination.

Cost-effectiveness would deal with another problem. The FDA banned sassafras tea on the grounds that it contained a carcinogen (safarole). Presumably none of the regulators drank sassafras tea, and thus all believed it to have no advantage over other teas and to have some small risk. It is doubtful that this tea is much, if at all, riskier than any other teas. But it was used by few people and thus had no sizable constituency to protest. Any setting of agency priorities would have excluded sassafras tea from regulation as being too small a health threat to warrant attention.

One of the myths concerning the regulatory budget is that this framework requires precise quantification of costs and health effects to be implemented. The four substances under consideration show this myth to be fallacious. Even a crude quantification of costs and health risks makes it apparent that aflatoxin is a higher priority issue than the other three. Furthermore, even crude quantification would probably show that other FDA actions would have more health benefit per dollar of control cost than would lowering tolerance levels for aflatoxin.

Benefit-Cost Analysis

This framework would go beyond the general balancing of effects by attempting to quantify all aspects of the problem and then by translating the effects into dollars.

135. Consumer surplus is a measure of the surplus, or additional, benefit of consuming a good above that needed to balance the social cost of producing the good. Economists estimate the area under the demand curve, above the current price, to be a rough approximation of how much more consumers would be willing to pay for a good than they currently pay. The assumptions required to make this approximation a rigorous measure are rarely met. In addition the measure depends critically on the current distribution of income and the availability of substitute and complementary products. Despite the difficulties, this notion of consumer surplus is extremely useful in practice.

Without nitrite, the taste and color of cured meats would be judged to be less appealing. Before writing such changes off as unimportant, one should consider how much is spent in the United States for products with better appearance or taste.[136] Economists would estimate the dollar value of this loss by using the concept of consumer surplus, implementing the technique by estimating demand functions for the current types of cured meats. (Actually, the demand would be somewhat lower if people were informed of the risk of nitrite, but this effect is likely to be small.) Since there have not been resources to estimate these demand schedules, one would merely note that the amount of consumer loss is large and likely to be measured in the tens of billions of dollars.[137] One might follow the Federal Aviation Administration in valuing a premature death at $300,000—perhaps any cancer would be valued at this amount.[138] An estimate is also needed for the social cost of a malformation due to DES. Virtually all congenital effects would be microscopic and would be expected to disappear over time; since they would not be perceived or have any effect, they could be disregarded. But some might be perceptible, reduce fertility, or reduce the chance of carrying a baby to term. The latter effects are likely to be rare, occurring perhaps in no more than a few percent of the women with malformations. Insofar as a woman cannot have the number of children she desires, this is a serious consequence. Since I cannot suggest a value for such an effect in which I have confidence, I

136. Various studies have been done of the lowest cost at which a diet with adequate calories, vitamins, and minerals could be purchased; for example, George J. Stigler, "The Cost of Subsistence," pp. 303–14. The answer is about $200 per person per year. This result suggests that Americans could spend less than $45 billion a year and obtain a nutritionally adequate diet. But they actually spend hundreds of billions of dollars on food. Thus only a tiny fraction of food expenditures are for basic nutrition, and the rest goes for appearance, taste, variety, and extra quantity. It is therefore apparent that regulation that ignores appearance and taste or treats them as worthless will lead to undesirable results.

137. I know of no demand schedule that has been estimated for cured meat, but assume that the demand function is a straight line with an elasticity of -0.65 at the current equilibrium. About 9 billion pounds of nitrite-cured meat (7 percent of the U.S. food supply) was sold in 1976 (see FDA and USDA, "FDA's and USDA's Action Regarding Nitrite," p. 6); assume this sold for an average of $2 a pound. Then the estimated loss in consumer surplus from banning nitrite would be $13.9 billion. Even if the price elasticity were as high as -1.5, the loss in consumer surplus would be $6 billion a year.

138. U.S. Department of Transportation, Federal Aviation Administration, *Establishment Criteria for Category I Instrument Landing System (ILS)*, p. B-8; and Robert S. Smith, "Compensating Wage Differentials and Public Policy: A Review," pp. 16–23.

pick a very high estimate that places an upper bound on the social cost of genital malformations. Since the majority of malformations disappear over time, and since only a small proportion of those women with malformations would experience difficulties, only a tiny number of women would be affected. Assuming each malformation costs society $50,000 means that the social cost would be many times this estimate for each woman who could not have all the children she desired or who had a perceptible malformation.

Using these values, one might tabulate the benefits of banning nitrite or DES and lowering the tolerance level of aflatoxin. Before doing that, I reiterate the crudeness of the data, difficulties in estimating effects, and problems even in establishing that these substances are human carcinogens. In all of the estimates that follow, the reader must recognize that each number could be wrong by a factor of two, or even ten, in either direction.

Benefit-cost analysis makes no contribution over previous frameworks in the evaluation of nitrite. The analysis done for the risk-risk framework indicates that banning nitrite could result in at least as many premature deaths as continuing to use it. The succeeding frameworks all tend to add to the costs of banning nitrite without providing any additional justification for banning it. Thus the additional quantification from benefit-cost analysis supports the decision that would be reached under a simpler framework by showing costs in addition to those associated with health risks.

Benefit-cost analysis is helpful for regulating aflatoxin, since options range from keeping the present standard to banning peanuts and corn production in the Southeast. Lowering tolerance levels below the current standard of 20 ppb appears to cost little and would be estimated to save lives, but the cost of lowering tolerance levels would be expected to increase rapidly at much lower levels.

Costs for reducing aflatoxin levels have not been estimated. This precludes a complete analysis, but it is possible to estimate the benefits of reducing aflatoxin levels in food. I again assume that each liver cancer costs society $300,000; the value of reducing aflatoxin exposure by 50 percent would be $11.4 million to $37.8 million a year since it would prevent 38–126 liver cancers a year.[139] Thus if the cost of reducing afla-

139. Aflatoxin is estimated to account for 2.4–7.9 percent of liver cancers, which is not implausible.

toxin exposures by 50 percent were less than $11.4 million to $37.8 million a year, the program would be worthwhile.

This example makes it apparent that even crude estimates of benefits and costs are often sufficient to form a basis for judgment. Even without cost estimation, a precise question can be posed. A relatively small amount of work should suffice to indicate whether it is conceivable that aflatoxin exposure can be lessened by 50 percent for an expenditure of $11.4 million to $37.8 million a year. Further, if costs can be estimated for various levels of reduced aflatoxin exposure, a program can be found in which the benefits of a small decrease in aflatoxin exposure is just equal to the costs of achieving it. Certainly the social cost of banning peanuts and corn production in the Southeast would be much greater than $22.8 million to $75.6 million a year, and so lowering risk as much as possible makes no sense.

Benefit-cost analysis is also helpful for saccharin, since health effects are to be balanced against the nonhealth benefits of having a nonnutritive sweetener. Current estimates of benefits and risks indicate that society is unlikely to ban saccharin, although it might want to lower consumption by children, pregnant women, and smokers.

The benefit-cost framework is perhaps most helpful in evaluating DES. As long as cancers and teratogenic effects are on one side of the scale and dollars, occupational accidents, disease, and environmental effects are on the other, a decision is difficult to reach. Only by implicitly or explicitly translating the health effects into dollars can the decision be made unambiguous. In the earlier discussion the cost of banning DES is estimated to be $523 million to $5 billion a year. The benefit of doing so is estimated to be a reduction in mammary tumors of 128 a year and in teratogenic effects of 3 a year.

At $300,000 per cancer (not all of which result in death) and $50,000 per teratogenic effect, this reduction in adverse health effects would be worth approximately $38.6 million a year. Even if the estimated effects or valuations were multiplied by 10, the benefit-cost framework makes it clear that DES should not be banned. An alternative way of looking at the issue is to assume that the average teratogenic effect costs society one-sixth as much as a mammary tumor (based on the ratio of $300,000 to $50,000) and then to calculate how much society would have to be willing to spend to prevent a cancer in order to justify banning DES. This analysis implies that society would have to be willing to spend at least

$3.9 million to $39 million per cancer and $0.65 million to $6.5 million per teratogenic effect in order for it to be rational to ban DES.[140]

Conclusion

The no-risk framework and technology-based standards are qualitatively different from the succeeding ones, all of which require at least some quantification of risk. These five examples clarify the difficulties in estimating risk:

1. The human data on dose and response are usually inadequate and even animal bioassay data are often inadequate. Even with perfect data one hesitates to extrapolate risks to 220 million Americans on the basis of a small number of rats divided into a control group and low- and high-dose groups. Risk estimates are unlikely to be accurate within 10 percent and possibly not even within a factor of ten. Care must be taken to estimate risk based on a range of assumptions, one end of which will almost surely overstate the true risk to humans and the other end, understate it.

2. Vast uncertainties remain in the biological models. In an animal bioassay, one should choose a species that is deemed to react to the substance in a way similar to humans. In making the risk extrapolation to humans, one must know at least a modicum about the mechanism by which cancer was induced to determine, for example, whether the extrapolation should be on the basis of dose per unit of body weight. Generally there is little confidence in either the choice of species or the extrapolation method.

3. Environmental insults tend to interact, often producing a combined result greater than the sum of the individual results. One chemical might "potentiate" or markedly enhance another or the two might join to overwhelm the body's defense mechanisms. Thus one can get only the crudest estimate of risk by considering one insult at a time.

4. Assuming that a uniform dose is applied to a homogeneous population may make the calculation simple, but it is highly inaccurate. Personal

140. The 128 mammary tumors and 3 malformations a year would be 128.5 cancer equivalents (assuming the malformations are equal to one-sixth of a cancer). Thus $5 billion divided by 128.5 is $38.9 million; the cost per malformation would be one-sixth of this amount, or $6.5 million. The conclusion neglects possible redistribution of income and counts occupational injury and disease as equivalent to consumer disease.

habits and work exposures differ among socioeconomic groups and areas of the country. For example, some groups eat large amounts of coho salmon from Lake Michigan with resulting abnormal exposure to PCBs. The genetic heterogeneity of the population means that some people are likely to be highly resistant to a chemical or biological insult and others highly sensitive;[141] for example, the log-probit model assumes that the underlying distribution of tolerances in the population is log-normal.

5. Given the imperfections of risk estimation, its usefulness is assessed through several questions. Is the conservative estimation procedure indeed conservative? What is the likelihood that the true risk is significantly greater than the conservative estimate? Can researchers learn from applying the technique and evaluating the outcome so that both the science and regulation will be improved? Although the difficulties are formidable, I believe that better public policy can be made on the basis of risk estimation than from a no-risk framework.

Another set of issues are commonly associated with the frameworks beyond no risk and cited as reasons for sticking to the simple framework. For example, equity issues are rarely considered explicitly in doing a benefit-cost analysis. At the same time, benefit-cost analysis requires decisions to be made for consumers that will put them at jeopardy or cost them money without giving them a real voice in the outcome. Finally, it is alleged that benefit-cost analysis requires the weighing of noncommensurate factors, such as lives and dollars.

All these statements are true, but they are equally true for all regulatory frameworks, including no-risk (except market regulation). Equity issues arise in each and are rarely considered. For example, banning swordfish causes fishermen to lose income and some people to have a less adequate diet. If anything, the comprehensiveness of benefit-cost analysis allows more explicit consideration of these issues. By definition, regulators make decisions for consumers, not consumers for themselves; only market regulation is responsive to the criticism of consumers. Finally, all frameworks require a weighing, implicitly or explicitly of noncommensurate factors. The no-risk framework assumes that one life or one illness is worth an arbitrarily large amount of economic resources. Obviously that is inconsistent with both individual and governmental decisions.

The appeal of the risk-risk framework is that it appears to be balancing

141. Gilbert S. Omenn and Robert D. Friedman, "Individual Differences in Susceptibility and Regulation of Environmental Hazards."

commensurates: lives against lives. The intuitive appeal of this approach cannot be dismissed, particularly since it was proposed by the FDA and the Department of Agriculture. Furthermore, at least in its indirect version, risk-risk analysis is a rough approximation to the more comprehensive frameworks, such as formal benefit-cost analysis. While these advantages are formidable, there is still the theoretical objection that it fails to take account of consumer preferences and gives almost no consideration to the economic costs of the regulation.

The informal balancing of benefits and risks, benefits and costs, does give consideration to all aspects of the problem. Since no procedures for analysis or evaluation are specified, however, these would have to be developed in the course of regulation. The difficulty with this informal procedure revolves around attempts to implement it within the U.S. administrative-legal system. Whatever the merits of incremental development for common law, it is not satisfactory for an analytical framework. One might picture a proceeding where an agency spent years listening to every possible effect that someone wanted to testify about. Tens or hundreds of thousands of pages of record would be delivered to the agency, all of which would have to be considered in arriving at a decision. One suspects a good challenge to an eventual decision would be that the agency could not possibly have considered all aspects during the period between the closing of the record and eventual decision.

Cost-effectiveness analysis is only as good as the statement of goals and estimation of the relevant benefits and costs. The estimates of costs and benefits need not be completely accurate as long as they are systematically biased upward or downward by a constant factor. The great advantage of cost-effectiveness analysis is that it forces a general view and setting of priorities.

The regulatory budget suffers from four difficulties. The first applies to cost-effectiveness as well; while costs and effects have to be estimated in each of these frameworks, doing the division in order to get an order of priorities requires confidence in the estimates. Surely one should group proposed regulations into general categories defined by the general cost-effectiveness of the group, rather than take seriously minor differences in cost-effectiveness.

The second difficulty is determining the regulatory budget for each agency. Given Congress's long experience in setting outlay budgets for agencies, it would not seem difficult to set an implementation or "cost to the private sector" budget. The whole budgeting process would be evolutionary, with the results of previous experience tempering the credibility of new requests and serving as a guide to the efficacy of funds for each agency.

The third difficulty is estimating the costs of implementation. The direct costs of a regulation could be quantified in terms of the immediate increases in costs, but second-order costs as well as opportunity costs are more difficult to quantify. At least initially, it seems likely that the agency would attempt to estimate only the direct costs. This, however, would push the agency toward changing its regulations so as to shift costs away from the direct category. For example, banning cured meats would have little direct costs (but very large opportunity costs), while requiring more stringent controls in the manufacturing process and transportation of cured meats would have large direct costs. Since there are ample opportunities for distorting regulations to shift costs out of the direct category, the regulatory budget approach could work only if estimates of indirect and opportunity costs were included.

The fourth and largest difficulty is jurisdiction. If a regulatory budget were given to the FDA, it would cover food, drugs, and cosmetics, with overlapping jurisdiction with the Department of Agriculture, Federal Trade Commission, and so forth. Congress might grow unhappy if the FDA felt that public health could be enhanced most by giving all its attention to drugs, with none for food or cosmetics. Jurisdictional disputes among agencies would be exacerbated. This objection has a sort of poetic justice about it since it would require Congress to correct some of the difficulties created by inattention to overlapping responsibilities.

The framework does not impose any new burdens on Congress or cause it to meddle in regulatory details. Congress already has oversight responsibility; the regulatory budget would merely sharpen and focus authority. With a clearer articulation of priorities, fewer occasions would arise when Congress would feel the necessity of instructing an agency about details.

Formal benefit-cost analysis is the most comprehensive of the frameworks and requires the most data, analysis, and definition of procedures. The framework calls on all the theoretical contributions from economics and the lessons from prior applications. It also runs afoul of incommensurates since it requires placing an explicit value on human life. The theoretical appeal of this framework is evident, but the practical difficulties in implementation are immense.

Of these various frameworks, I find the regulatory budget most appealing. First, it explicitly forces agencies to sort out their priorities and to articulate and defend them annually before Congress. Furthermore, the feedback mechanism (bringing together previous estimates of risks and costs with the actual experience) would help to keep agencies honest and sharp. This framework does not require an explicit value on human life, which is no small advantage. Finally, it focuses attention on some of the underlying reasons for the regulatory muddle, such as the overlapping jurisdiction of agencies. Most important, it forces Congress and the administration to articulate broad policy in a fashion that is understandable to the average voter; it focuses the debate on the right questions.

CHAPTER FIVE

Health, Safety, and Environmental Regulations

THE UNITED STATES is a nation governed by law, with judicial review of the laws and, more pertinently, of the decisions of regulatory agencies. Regulation cannot be arbitrary and capricious. Rather, the decision frameworks and process for making a regulation must be set out carefully and applied uniformly. Each regulatory agency must have operational goals and a set of rules for estimating risks and benefits. Even a coherent and complete decision framework would be useless for regulatory decisionmaking unless it could be applied routinely using available data, codified practices, and civil servant analysts.

Carcinogenic food additives, discussed in chapter 4, are perhaps the most difficult area for the application of the eight decision frameworks. The scientific foundation for estimating the risks from minute doses of carcinogens is missing and value conflicts dominate.

Before examining other health and safety regulations, it is illuminating to present a quite different example. In defense policy the goal (defense or deterrence) is not measurable. Although defense policy wallows in uncertainty and in the inability to quantify many of the important aspects, analyses of alternatives have become essential to policy formulation. A defense force of current size and complexity could not be planned, trained, and deployed without sophisticated analysis. Modern military analysis began with President Kennedy's secretary of defense, Robert MacNamara, and his comptroller, Charles Hitch, who attempted to apply quantitative analysis in support of virtually all major decisions.[1] While they experienced major failures (when their analysis was distracting or even harmful), their cost-effectiveness analysis helped improve the efficiency of defense. Since analysis has played an invaluable role in the com-

1. Charles J. Hitch and Roland N. McKean, *The Economics of Defense in the Nuclear Age.*

plicated and controversial area of defense policy, presumably it can help improve health and safety decisions.

Analyses of various areas of social regulation—occupational health and safety, the environment, health, transport safety, and consumer products—will be reviewed in this chapter, and the special difficulties for analysis in each area will be discussed. Four case studies will be considered and the eight decision frameworks will be applied to each: occupational disease among coke oven workers, photochemical oxidant air pollution, frangible light standards for airports, and passive restraints for automobile occupants. The chapter focuses on answering three questions. Is there a scientific basis for analyzing the risk of exposure to toxic substances and accident hazards? How do uncertainties in the analysis and ignorance of aspects of the scientific foundation affect conclusions? Can analyses in each area offer insights for regulatory decisionmaking?

Occupational Health and Safety

The creation of the National Institute of Occupational Safety and Health and of the Occupational Safety and Health Administration (OSHA) in 1970 gave a large push to the field of occupational health.[2] Prognostic studies that quantify the health experience of workers have been done for such industries as steel, coal mining, rubber, and textiles.[3] Excess risks (that is, those that are larger than the risks of "normal" activity) are estimated in an attempt to identify the overall level of risk and to isolate hazardous substances or working conditions. Quantitative estimates of risk have been used, principally by critics, in considering OSHA standards for coke ovens, cotton dust, inorganic arsenic, benzene, and other hazards. These risk estimates provide an important component of the estimated benefit of a regulation.

Determinants of Occupational Disease

Epidemiological studies in general and occupational studies in particular are invariably controversial. A good study must observe the dose

2. Linnea Freeburg, "Epidemiological Studies in Occupational Health: An Annotated Bibliography."

3. U.S. Department of Health, Education, and Welfare, National Institutes of Health, *Human Health and the Environment: Some Research Needs,* pp. 55–70; and Donald V. Lassiter, "Occupational Carcinogenesis," pp. 63–86.

from a toxic chemical and the resulting effect on health status, and it must control, explicitly or statistically, factors that might cause the response, including personal habits, family history, and exposures to other toxic substances. Finally, the study must contrast the study population with an appropriate control group and must have a large enough population to obtain significant conclusions.

Subtle biases can creep in unintentionally. For example, a researcher may hear of an unusually high incidence of some disease in the workers of a plant and decide to select it for study. However, if the study group is selected because of prestudy information that the response was particularly high in this group, disease incidence will be correlated with exposure as a result of selection bias, even in cases where there is no causal relationship. Many study conclusions are invalid under such conditions. Epidemiological studies of chronic disease require observations of dose and response over a number of years, or even decades, but it is nearly impossible to observe dose for each individual over decades. At best one can attempt to characterize the general nature of exposure in each year by the location of the worker and by the dose associated with his job. Unfortunately lack of data or data of poor quality prevents dose estimation from being accurate. For example, air quality has deteriorated and then improved in major cities and varies from area to area within the city; thus, what dose has a sixty-year-old urbanite received?

Similarly, response is poorly measured, with time and cause of death being the parameters most often used. Death certificates are notoriously inaccurate concerning both the immediate cause of death and the number of diseases contributing to death. An alternative is to use physical examinations or patient reports of health status. Patient reports are inaccurate because individual perceptions differ regarding what constitutes an incapacitating condition and when the first significant symptoms appeared. Physical examinations focus on the physician's perception of the patient's condition, which may have little relationship to pain or incapacity. For example, coal workers' pneumoconiosis (black lung) has been controversial because chest pain or shortness of breath may occur without medical evidence of progressive massive fibrosis.[4] Congress felt that medical evidence of pneumoconiosis was too stringent a criterion for

4. National Academy of Sciences, *Mineral Resources and the Environment, Supplementary Report, Coal Worker Pneumoconiosis—Medical Considerations, Some Social Implications*, pp. 4–15.

qualifying for federal benefits and permitted respiratory symptoms to be used as well.

The environment contains thousands of toxic substances; even the most important ones are difficult to measure, much less control.[5] How much of the incidence or severity of chronic disease is due to occupational exposure? To the general environment? To personal habits? Confounding current measures of exposure is past exposure to toxic substances in another occupation or in the general environment. The most important environmental toxin many workers are exposed to is tobacco smoke; without controlling for cigarette smoking, it is difficult to make inferences about the prevalence of cardiovascular disease, respiratory disease, or cancer. Other personal habits, including nutritional history, exercise history, and whether a person is overweight, are important factors determining health status. Individual susceptibility (as measured by family health history) is another factor affecting the prevalence of disease.[6]

It is impossible to control, explicitly or statistically, for all these factors. The situation that comes closest to doing so is an animal bioassay in which inbred (genetically homogeneous) animals are exposed to a toxic substance under carefully controlled conditions. An occupational setting for humans is not even a remote approximation to an animal bioassay. Each occupational health study is attacked because some of these aspects are not controlled in the analysis and others are inadequately controlled.

The distressing possibility always remains that personal habits or genetic background are systematically related to the occupation under study, as when a homogeneous ethnic group holds a particular set of jobs, such as working in a steel mill or coal mine. Some of these problems can be handled by obtaining a population sufficiently large to support the expectation that variations in personal habits would average out. Moreover, the sample must be large enough to permit obtaining statistically significant comparisons. This is often difficult because only a few people are in a particular type of job.

The selection of an appropriate control group is important in that changes in the composition of the group can alter the significance, and even the sign, of observed effects. For example, the cardiovascular mor-

5. Chemical substances that are either currently controlled or slated for control appear in U.S. Office of Technology Assessment, "Assessment of Technologies for Determining Cancer Risks from the Environment" (February 1981), chap. 7.

6. Gilbert S. Omenn and Robert D. Friedman, "Individual Differences in Susceptibility and Regulation of Environmental Hazards."

tality rate of one set of workers might be high relative to that of a set of blue-collar workers who perform strenuous work but low relative to that of a set of white-collar workers who receive less exercise. Ideally the control and study groups should be identical except for the exposure. In practice a large element of judgment is involved in selecting a comparable control group. Since study funds are limited, the control group is likely to be either readily available or a group that has been studied for other reasons.

All these difficulties are less formidable when workers experience high incidence of a disease owing to high exposure—for example, angiosarcoma from vinyl chloride.[7] While major effects eliminate doubt concerning the existence of excess risk, they do not provide assurance that the observed association is causal (was it the vinyl chloride or some other chemical that produced the liver cancer?) and provide little evidence on the dose-response relationship. For example, some scientists contend that cigarette smoking has not been shown to cause lung cancer; furthermore, they maintain that the epidemiological studies are so flawed that they cannot be used to estimate the magnitude of effect, even if cigarette smoking did cause lung cancer.[8]

Coke Oven Workers: A Case Study

Many of the difficulties in conducting and interpreting occupational health studies are illustrated by a large, prognostic study known as the Long-Term Mortality Study of Steelworkers.[9] This study drew a sample

7. David D. Doniger, *The Law and Policy of Toxic Substances Control: A Case Study of Vinyl Chloride.*

8. Theodor D. Sterling, "A Critical Reassessment of the Evidence Bearing on Smoking as the Cause of Lung Cancer," pp. 939–53; William Weiss, "Smoking and Cancer: A Rebuttal," pp. 954–55; Ian T. T. Higgins, "Commentary: Smoking and Cancer," pp. 159–60; and Theodor D. Sterling, "Additional Comments on the Critical Assessment of the Evidence Bearing on Smoking as the Cause of Lung Cancer," pp. 161–63.

9. J. William Lloyd and Antonio Ciocco, "Long-Term Mortality Study of Steelworkers," pt. 1: "Methodology," pp. 299–310; Harry Robinson, "Long-Term Mortality Study of Steelworkers," pt. 2: "Mortality by Level of Income in Whites and Non-Whites," pp. 411–16; Carol K. Redmond and others, "Long-Term Mortality Study of Steelworkers," pt. 3: "Follow-Up," pp. 513–21; J. William Lloyd, "Long-Term Mortality Study of Steelworkers," pt. 4: "Mortality by Work Area," pp. 151–60; Lloyd, "Long-Term Mortality Study of Steelworkers," pt. 5: "Respiratory Cancer in Coke Plant Workers," pp. 53–68; and Carol K. Redmond and others, "Long-Term Mortality Study of Steelworkers," pt. 6: "Mortality from Malignant Neoplasms among Coke Oven Workers," pp. 621–29.

of workers employed in steel facilities as of 1953.[10] Work histories were obtained for the study population and workers have been followed over the succeeding years. An extensive analysis of occupational disease due to coke oven exposure was performed using the date and cause of death obtained from the death certificate of each former worker.

The study design is important in defining the type of data available and the nature of the conclusions that can be drawn. Since the vast majority of workers in the sample had been employed in the steel industry for more than one year at the beginning of the study, virtually all were men in robust good health without severe allergies or cardiovascular or respiratory conditions that would have limited their activity. Workers with such conditions would not have been attracted to the steel industry and, of those who secured jobs, few would have survived the first days of strenuous activity and difficult work conditions. This group is not typical of the population or even of the work force in general. Inferences can be drawn only about men in robust good health at the time of initial employment. For example, the study found that steelworkers had a lower incidence of cardiovascular disease than did the population generally, a not unexpected result.

Since the study design did not involve worker interviews or physical examinations, important information is unavailable. Employment records do not contain such data as smoking habits and family history of chronic disease. Without physical examinations or interviews concerning health status, the only health outcomes available to the study were time and cause of death.

Early in the study it became apparent that coke oven workers had lung cancer mortality rates that were much higher than those in the population generally or among other steelworkers. This association was plausible because of the toxic brew of carcinogens in coke oven emissions, especially the coal tars such as benzo-(a)-pyrene. Since the study focused on lung cancer, the failure to collect data on cigarette smoking was critical; if coke oven workers were especially heavy smokers the observed association might be due only to cigarette smoking. This suspicion was not put to rest until the analysis demonstrated that the rate of lung cancer was higher than could be explained by heavy smoking alone. Even so, the dose-response relationship cannot be estimated with confidence without knowledge of the workers' smoking habits.

10. This section relies on Dwight D. Briggs and Lester B. Lave, "Risk Assessments of Coke Oven Emissions."

Obtaining data on the number (and cause) of deaths of workers from death certificates creates a problem. Some workers migrate to other areas or even leave the United States; thus investigators must cull local and national death records to learn if any of the workers have died. Failure to locate a worker leads to an underestimate of the mortality rate and produces biased estimates. The usual difficulties with the recorded cause of death are confounded by regional differences in assigning cause of death and completeness of the report. Small biases are important for relatively rare causes of death.

Problems in measuring response (longevity and cause of death) are matched by problems in determining dose. It is impossible to recreate the dose of carcinogens received by each worker during his employment. Few measurements of the concentrations of coal tar pitch volatiles were taken in the 1940s and 1950s. The small number of measurements are not necessarily representative of the exposure of all workers or of any one worker over time in the plant sampled, due to changes in the coal used, maintenance procedures, or new equipment. At best, a crude index of exposure can be constructed from the location and type of job for each worker. Those working beside the oven received greater doses than those working at a distance. Measured concentrations at each location can be used to define an exposure index by weighting the number of months spent at each job location by the concentration of carcinogens at that location. Needless to say, this exposure index will be only a crude measure of actual dose.

The importance of the difficulties in measuring dose and response, personal habits, and other exposures is shown by comparing the Long-Term Mortality Study of Steelworkers with one done on British coke oven workers by Reid and Buck.[11] In contrast to the American long-term study, the British one shows no rise in lung cancer risk. When the two studies are compared, however, the British study can be seen to be the least satisfactory. The sample size is smaller and workers were followed for a shorter time; dose was measured more crudely, with no attempt to use work location to indicate dose. The control group was not defined well; hence the failure to find higher risk among coke oven workers might be due to the high lung cancer risk in the control group.

The American study was superior in sample design and analysis, and its results should be accepted over those of the British study. Nonetheless,

11. D. D. Reid and Carol L. Buck, "Cancer in Coking Plant Workers," pp. 265–69.

the results of the American study remain controversial. The magnitudes of the estimated dose-response relationship are influenced by patterns of cigarette smoking, family history of chronic disease, and previous work exposures. But securing the information needed to separate effects is expensive (since an interview and possibly a physical examination are needed), difficult (because of worker suspicion that the answers will affect continued employment or promotion), and raises ethical issues (as when the history or examination reveals information suggesting a person will face a higher risk if he continues to be employed in this industry).[12] What legal or ethical obligations exist to suggest that the worker needs medical treatment or a different job?

Assuming that the number of cancers among the workers is known, that the work history is accurate and provides a reasonable estimate of the dose, and that the measurements of coal tar pitch volatiles characterize the relevant set of coke ovens for the relevant period of time, one has the basic data for estimating a dose-response relationship.[13] It should be evident, however, that all the variables are subject to large errors of measurement and that the number of data points to be used in the estimation is small.[14] Many different dose-response curves fit the data about equally well, and these different curves have very different implications concerning the amount of lung cancer that would be expected if exposure were lowered.[15] Neither underlying knowledge of biology and human physiology nor careful analysis of the data is capable of singling out one dose-response curve as better than another. A judgment is required in choosing among the various curves and their very different implications concerning the expected incidence of lung cancer exposure levels.

In addition to the functional form of the dose-response relationship, an assumption must be made concerning the lag between exposure and the occurrence of lung cancer. The cancer is not produced instantaneously. There is some evidence from the study suggesting that the lag is on the

12. For example, cigarette-smoking asbestos workers are at many times the risk of nonsmoking workers. Irving J. Selikoff, E. Cuyler Hammond, and Jacob Churq, "Asbestos Exposure, Smoking, and Neoplasia," pp. 104–10. The Johns Mansville Company has attempted to keep cigarette smokers from asbestos exposure.

13. Charles E. Land, "Informal Public Hearing Re: Proposed Standard for Coke Oven Emissions," pp. 3853–58.

14. There were less than two dozen workers in the high exposure group of the long-term mortality study.

15. Land, "Informal Public Hearing." See also Sati Mazumdar and Carol K. Redmond, "Evaluating Dose-Response Relationships Using Epidemiological Data on Occupational Subgroups," pp. 275–81.

order of twenty to thirty years.[16] Land estimated the relationships assuming lags of zero, five, ten, and fifteen years; the last led to a much lower effect than the assumption of no lag or one of five years.[17]

While there are a host of problems in establishing that coke oven emissions cause lung cancer and in estimating the quantitative response, at least rough quantification is provided by this series of studies. The relationship is sufficiently strong to dismiss objections about uncontrolled factors, although they may still affect the dose-response estimates. This work provided a basis for a rough estimate of the effects of different standards by OSHA and for draft regulations by the Environmental Protection Agency (EPA).

The eight decision frameworks could be applied to this case. OSHA lowered permissible concentration of coal tar pitch volatiles in the air from 0.2 to 0.15 milligram per cubic meter, stopping at this level because of uncertainty about technology and the ability of the industry to bear these costs, even though it estimated the standard would leave coke oven workers at elevated risk of lung cancer. The EPA proposes to set a standard for general population exposure to these emissions.

Market regulation would call for publicizing the results of these studies to workers and their union. Individual workers would then be free to seek new jobs, their union would have information to use in collective bargaining, and workers dying of lung cancer could sue their employer for compensation. Given the likely success of such suits and the strength of the union, steel companies would probably proceed to attain lower emission levels.

The no-risk framework would call for shutting coke ovens unless emissions could be reduced to zero. This solution was not proposed by OSHA, EPA, or the United Steelworkers of America. Management and labor would presumably join together to fight closing coke ovens.

Technology-based standards would call for best available control technology. While there is some dispute about the availability of technology that will meet the OSHA standards, a case can be made that even better control technology is currently available. Thus OSHA set a standard less stringent than best available control technology, presumably because it felt the industry could not afford a more stringent standard.

Risk-risk is not applicable since there is no opposing risk to workers that might offset that from coke oven emissions.

16. Redmond and others, "Long-Term Mortality Study of Steelworkers," pt. 6.
17. Land, "Informal Public Hearing."

Risk-benefit analysis helps little, as the trade-off between the price of steel and the risk to coke oven workers is complicated. A conventional approach is to examine the risk to these workers in relation to risks to other workers. Certainly the risk to workers spending more than a decade at jobs on the top of the oven is very high, probably unacceptably high, and lowering their risk to the level of all workers would require stringent standards. No explicit proposal comes from this framework, however.

Cost-effectiveness and the regulatory budget would require OSHA to compare the risks associated with coke oven emissions with those of other areas under its jurisdiction. OSHA actions could save lives at lower cost in other areas, such as cotton plants, but the risk to each worker of lung cancer and premature death is much greater for workers with jobs on the top of coke ovens. These frameworks could be used to set a specific standard, given the opportunities for preventing premature death in other occupations.

Benefit-cost analysis was used implicitly in setting the regulation. Considerable dispute arose about the costs of meeting this standard and some dispute about the number of lung cancers that would be prevented.[18] OSHA was challenged by the Council on Wage and Price Stability, which asserted that the cost per life saved was too great to justify the current regulation.[19] The council proposed that work rules be changed to limit the exposure of coke oven workers by rotating them to other jobs; this would spread the risk among more workers but would not lower the total number of lung cancers (assuming a linear dose-response function). The point of this proposal was that the regulation was not cost-effective, although someone working on the top of a coke oven for two decades would be subject to an unacceptable risk. The council's proposal would lower the risk for every person to an acceptable level and then would focus attention on the overall standard that would be cost-effective.

Other Occupational Studies

Other OSHA regulations concern exposure to many substances, including vinyl chloride, lead, benzene, cotton dust, and arsenic.[20] In each

18. "Exposure to Coke Oven Emissions," *Federal Register,* vol. 41 (October 22, 1976), pp. 46748–51.
19. James C. Miller III, "Exposure to Coke Oven Emissions Proposed Standard."
20. Richard A. Merrill, "Federal Regulation of Cancer-Causing Chemicals," chap. 4: "OSHA Regulation of Toxic Chemicals in the Workplace"; Richard Zeck-

case the standard-setting process has developed data on dose and response, leading to at least rough estimates of the incidence of disease that would be expected from alternative exposure levels.

The effect of cotton dust on lung function is not controversial, nor is the dose-response relationship—within a range accounting for uncertainty.[21] Controversy revolved around the cost of proposed regulations, the amount that society ought to be willing to spend to prevent a case of byssinossis (brown lung), and the precise standards for each aspect of production and storage. Morrall claims that the standards could have been more cost-effective by tightening them in areas where it is cheap to control cotton dust and ignoring them where control is expensive;[22] a revised standard could have prevented more cases of brown lung at a lower social cost. Such a standard, however, would have left some workers exposed to high levels of cotton dust and thus at high risk. Equity issues appear to have been important enough to OSHA to have dominated cost-effectiveness.

Although OSHA and the other social regulatory agencies have been challenged repeatedly in court, the first case to be considered by the Supreme Court was OSHA's regulation of occupational exposure to benzene.[23] Benzene causes various blood disorders, the most serious of which is leukemia, at exposure levels in excess of 100 parts per million. It has not been found to cause leukemia in animal bioassays.[24] There is some suggestion that benzene may cause leukemia at lower levels of exposure, possibly levels of 30 to 50 parts per million, but there is controversy over exposure levels and the incidence of leukemia. In 1977 OSHA lowered permissible exposure to benzene from 10 ppm to 1 ppm on the grounds that no one can be sure that any level of exposure to a carcinogen is safe and that the industry could afford the costs of implementing the rule.

hauser and Albert Nichols, "The Occupational Safety and Health Administration: An Overview," pp. 163–249; and Nicholas A. Ashford, *Crisis in the Workplace: Occupational Injury and Disease.*

21. James A. Merchant, "Byssinosis"; Morton Corn, "Regulation of Cotton Dust in Industry: The Regulatory Viewpoint"; and John F. Morrall III, "An Economic Analysis of OSHA's Cotton Dust Standard"; all in Robert W. Crandall and Lester B. Lave, eds., *The Scientific Basis of Health and Safety Regulations;* and U.S. Department of Labor, "Report to the Congress—Cotton Dust: Review of Alternative Technical Standards and Control Technologies," Draft (March 17, 1979), app. A.

22. Morrall, "An Economic Analysis of OSHA's Cotton Dust Standard."

23. Merrill, "Federal Regulation of Cancer-Causing Chemicals," chap. 4.

24. Thomas R. Bartman, "Benzene."

During the rule-making hearing this OSHA view was attacked by the presentation of quantitative risk analysis (done by a private party) that showed that the proposed reduction in benzene levels would lead to a minuscule reduction in risk.[25] Subsequently the EPA presented a quantitative risk analysis for benzene, which OSHA also found unconvincing.[26] OSHA rejected these analyses, arguing that the data were too incomplete to allow estimation of risk.[27]

The American Petroleum Institute challenged the regulation, and the Fifth Circuit Court of Appeals held that OSHA had failed to show that there would be an appreciable benefit to workers from this reduction in exposure level and argued that OSHA's statute required it to show that the benefits of a regulation were commensurate with the costs.[28] In July 1980 the Supreme Court issued its ruling on the case.[29] The court was divided, with four justices voting to overturn the lower court and uphold OSHA, four justices upholding the lower court on the grounds that OSHA had an obligation to show that an appreciable health benefit would result from the regulation, and one justice voting to uphold the lower court, arguing that the Occupational Safety and Health Act delegated so much authority to the agency that it was unconstitutional. The majority warned against an interpretation of the act that would allow the agency to make a broad declaration of policy, such as a uniform treatment of carcinogens, since this type of interpretation would probably be unconstitutional. The court specifically decided not to address the finding of the lower court that benefits and costs had to be at least roughly commensurate.

Although the acts of each of the social regulatory agencies differ, the Supreme Court seemed to warn the agencies that they must at least find an appreciable health benefit before promulgating a regulation. The court commented especially on the notion of striving for zero risk, saying that this was neither possible nor desirable.[30]

25. Richard Wilson, "Direct Testimony: Proposed Standards for Occupational Exposure to Benzene."

26. U.S. Environmental Protection Agency, *Assessment of Health Effects of Benzene Germane to Low-Level Exposure;* and U.S. Environmental Protection Agency, *Assessment of Human Exposures to Atmospheric Benzene.*

27. *Industrial Union Department, AFL-CIO* v. *American Petroleum Institute et al.,* brief for the federal parties in the Supreme Court (1979).

28. *Industrial Union Department, AFL-CIO* v. *American Petroleum Institute et al.,* 581 F. 2d 493 (5th Cir., 1978).

29. *AFL-CIO* v. *American Petroleum Institute et al.,* 48 U.S.L. Week 5022.

30. Ibid., p. 13.

The cases indicate that OSHA tried to protect worker health without worrying about costs or other factors. With respect to benzene, for which OSHA seems to have used a best-available-control-technology framework, the Supreme Court reversed the agency for not showing an appreciable risk and the appeals court asserted that benefits had to be roughly commensurate with costs. This review of the various cases shows that the more general frameworks can be applied to occupational health; the narrow frameworks, such as no risk or technology-based standards, will result in regulations that are inefficient and ineffective.

Regulating Occupational Safety

OSHA was created in part as a response to an increase in occupational accidents during the 1960s. Initially OSHA focused its efforts on reducing occupational accidents, particularly for a target set of industries. Unfortunately the Occupational Safety and Health Act of 1970 changed the accident reporting system; injury data before 1970 are not comparable with those for 1971 and later years. Thus no powerful tests of the hypothesis that OSHA lowered accident rates are possible. A series of weak tests, however, could uncover a substantial effect if one had occurred.

Several investigations of the effect of the act on occupational health have been performed. Smith analyzed the relationship between injury rates before and after the act in each industry, hypothesizing that regulation and inspections should have had the most effect on industries targeted for the greatest attention.[31] He found that injury rates tended to rise in these targeted industries relative to all others, although the result is not significant statistically.

Mendeloff, using a slightly different model and more recent data, also got insignificant results, but using California data and focusing on preventable accidents, he obtained significant results.[32] Because California had a strong occupational safety and health program both before OSHA and after 1970, it would not be expected to have had much of an improvement. Thus Mendeloff does not supply convincing evidence that OSHA lowered the accident rate. DiPietro used data on individual firms, by industry and firm size, to investigate whether recent inspections tended to

31. Robert Stewart Smith, *The Occupational Safety and Health Act: Its Goals and Its Achievements,* pp. 99 and 102.

32. John Mendeloff, "An Evaluation of the OSHA Program's Effect on Workplace Injury Rates: Evidence from California through 1974."

lower accident rates.[33] Most of her results are insignificant, and those that are significant have at least as many positive as negative signs. While plausible explanations can be offered for why OSHA inspections should be found to increase the observed accident rate, the fact remains that analysis fails to uncover convincing evidence that OSHA has succeeded in lowering the accident rate.

These studies provide a devastating critique of OSHA's efforts to improve occupational safety, indicating that OSHA had little or no effect on accident rates, even in targeted industries where its resources were focused. If these analyses had been done during the second and third year of the program, the failure would have led either to improved methods or to shifting resources toward lowering occupational disease.

Several lessons can be drawn from this case. The first is the penalty associated with the change in the way accident statistics were to be reported that occurred with the creation of the new agency. This step delayed analysis for several years and impeded efforts to manage the agency. The second is the agency's failure to respond to this change in statistical reporting by developing alternative time series that would have allowed it to monitor its efforts. Specific firms could have been asked to continue reporting data on the old (as well as the new) basis, and other firms could have been asked to apply the new reporting system to data from several years of history so that comparisons could be made. The third is that the criteria used for judging results were inadequate. Results were judged by the number of safety inspections and the number of violations cited, rather than by changes in accident rates. Thus the agency had little or no interest in monitoring its efforts to ensure that its goals were being accomplished. Even now no evidence shows that the agency is attempting to use its resources to accomplish the goals of lowering occupational accidents and disease in an effective manner.

The case studies show that the more general frameworks, from cost-effectiveness through benefit-cost analysis can be applied to occupational health and that they provide insights for decisionmaking. They push aside some issues as irrelevant and focus attention on the most important ones. More important, they show that the failure to apply these frameworks and to use their results to guide agency activity impaired the effectiveness of the agency in deploying resources and helped to prevent OSHA from achieving social goals in this area.

33. Aldona DiPietro, "An Analysis of the OSHA Inspection Program in Manufacturing Industries, 1972–1973," pp. 67–71.

Environment

Some government programs have undergone benefit-cost analysis since the 1930s, when the Army Corps of Engineers began evaluating waterway projects. The long history should not be assumed to reflect good analyses, however. Data often were gathered haphazardly and analyzed badly; there was intense pressure for the analysis to corroborate political decisions, and analysts at times have been asked to use their prestige to add respectability to political pork barrels. Recently the EPA published analyses of the benefits and costs of its air and water pollution programs, and a large literature exists of nongovernmental analyses.[34] The mistakes and pressures are still present, but the quality of environmental analyses can be high.

Photochemical Oxidants

The Clean Air Act Amendments of 1970 required EPA to set primary air quality standards that would protect the health of the population (presumably of even the most sensitive members). The level of 0.08 ppm established for photochemical oxidants in the 1971 standard was based on studies that seemed to show increases in asthma attacks and eye irritation down to perhaps 0.15 ppm.[35] EPA was required to review this standard in 1979. Since few studies had been done between 1971 and 1979, EPA was forced to concentrate on a reexamination of the studies used to set the earlier standard. Difficulties in measuring total oxidants led to setting the standard for ozone alone, and a close look at the studies led to a looser standard. In the midst of intense controversy EPA changed the standard from 0.08 ppm (total oxidants) to 0.12 ppm (ozone alone). Initially EPA proposed to reduce the standard to 0.10 ppm but decided to relax it further in view of criticism of the health studies on which it was based and the cost of controlling oxidants. Even so, EPA has been challenged in court, both by environmentalists wanting a more stringent stan-

34. U.S. Environmental Protection Agency, *The Cost of Clean Air and Water;* U.S. Environmental Protection Agency, *The Cost of Clean Air,* Report to Congress (EPA, August 1974); Allen V. Kneese and Blair T. Bower, *Environmental Quality and Residuals Management;* and Henry M. Peskin and Eugene P. Seskin, eds., *Cost Benefit Analysis and Water Pollution Policy.*
35. For a discussion of photochemical oxidants see Christopher Marraro, "The Revision of the Photochemical Oxidant (Ozone) Standard."

dard and by an industry group contending that the standard is more stringent than can be justified.

Ozone is a pulmonary irritant that affects respiratory mucous membranes, lung tissues, and respiratory functions.[36] A series of laboratory experiments indicates respiratory effects at concentrations of about 0.30 ppm and higher, although reactions are sensitive to the presence of other pollutants and to activity level. Epidemiological studies suggest reactions such as eye irritation, increased risk of asthma attacks, and respiratory symptoms at lower concentrations, down perhaps to 0.15 ppm.

One of the laboratory studies relied on by EPA in 1979, that by DeLucia and Adams, subjected six healthy, nonsmoking males to exposures of 0.15 or 0.30 ppm of ozone for one hour while at rest and while exercising at various levels of effort, including one so strenuous that some subjects had difficulty in completing the experiment.[37] Ozone was administered through a mouthpiece system that complicated breathing during strenuous exercise. While other experiments have used more satisfactory exposure devices, the difficulty and cost of the experiments have necessitated small, possibly unrepresentative samples.[38] None of the DeLucia and Adams subjects experienced any respiratory difficulties or symptoms when at rest, but they were uncomfortable during the most vigorous exercise at both ozone levels. Because of difficulties in experimental technique, however, the ozone levels could have been much higher than called for in the experimental design, and thus the effects could be due to higher doses. The discomfort disappeared shortly after the termination of the experiment.

Other laboratory studies must cope with the difficulty of small, not necessarily representative, numbers of subjects. Pure ozone does not seem to affect people at concentrations below 0.30 ppm unless they are exercising so strenuously that the symptoms could be due to the exercise itself. Some researchers have observed effects at lower concentrations since even trace amounts of other air pollutants, particularly sulfur oxides, seem to produce reactions. Finally, there appears to be a long-term adjustment to ozone levels; persons chronically exposed to elevated ozone pollution

36. Bernard David Goldstein, "Experimental and Clinical Problems of Effects of Photochemical Pollutants."

37. Anthony J. DeLucia and William C. Adams, "Effects of O_3 Inhalation during Exercise on Pulmonary Function and Blood Biochemistry," pp. 75–81.

38. Marraro, "The Revision of the Photochemical Oxidant (Ozone) Standard"; and Goldstein, "Experimental and Clinical Problems of Effects of Photochemical Pollutants."

levels are not as sensitive to increases in ozone as subjects are who have been breathing less polluted air.

The laboratory studies provide no evidence of health effects below a level of perhaps 0.30 ppm. It is customary and prudent, however, to choose a level lower than that at which effects are observed to serve as the standard. Whether this level should be two-thirds, one-half, or one-third the level at which health effects are observed is not evident. In this case the effects observed at high concentrations seem to occur only with strenuous exercise and to be transitory; if these are the only physiological effects, a small safety factor would seem adequate.

In setting the oxidant standard in 1971 the EPA relied on an epidemiological study by Schoettlin and Landau.[39] One hundred and fifty-seven patients being treated for bronchial asthma were selected as subjects because asthmatics were believed to be more sensitive to air pollution than the general population. During a three-month period participating subjects sent a form letter to their physicians reporting each asthma attack and giving details on severity, time of onset, and geographical location. The level of oxidant measured at the station closest to the geographical location was then related to each observed asthma attack, and a statistical analysis of the association between air pollution and asthma attack rates was performed. Between 6 and 14 percent of the variation in asthma attack rates was explained by various measures of oxidant level. No significant increase in asthma attacks occurred for days with oxidant levels over 0.13 ppm, but a significant increase for days with oxidant levels over 0.25 ppm was found.

Like the other epidemiological researchers studying the effects of oxidants, Schoettlin and Landau failed to observe or control (statistically) other factors hypothesized to be associated with asthma attacks, including other air pollutants, temperature, and certain days of the week.[40] All these factors are systematically associated with oxidant levels in Los Angeles. The worst smog occurs during periods of intense solar radiation when there is a temperature inversion in the atmosphere and increased emissions; associated with such conditions are high temperatures, high concentrations of other pollutants, and weekday business activity. Given this

39. Charles E. Schoettlin and Emanuel Landau, "Air Pollution and Asthmatic Attacks in the Los Angeles Area," pp. 545–48.
40. Marraro, "The Revision of the Photochemical Oxidant (Ozone) Standard," p. 19; and Lester B. Lave and Eugene P. Seskin, *Air Pollution and Human Health*, app. A.

host of simultaneous assaults on health, the study can be interpreted as indicating that asthmatics are certainly not sensitive to oxidants at levels of 0.13 ppm, and possibly not at levels up to 0.25 ppm; but at 0.25 ppm, oxidants and other factors (including temperature, other pollutants, and day of the week) are associated with an increase in asthma attacks.

The epidemiological literature adds little to the laboratory studies. There is no firm evidence of health effects below levels of 0.25 and 0.30 ppm. This is not to say that there are no health effects but merely that a number of attempts to demonstrate such an association using laboratory and epidemiological methods have failed. Confronted with this evidence, the EPA proposed to loosen the oxidant standard from 0.08 ppm of total oxidants to 0.10 ppm of ozone (measuring only ozone rather than total oxidant was also a slight relaxation of the standard). The EPA noted that it was also considering 0.12 ppm as a possible standard.[41]

More than a dozen cities are frequent violators of the 0.08 ppm standard and most would violate the 0.12 ppm one.[42] Vigorous enforcement would be needed to comply with stringent emission standards in the range of 0.16 to 0.20 ppm for cities located far enough south to have intense solar radiation and for those with considerable automobile traffic.

The Council on Wage and Price Stability analysis concluded that the standard should be in the range of 0.16 to 0.20 ppm.[43] The council estimated that the incremental costs associated with achieving standards in the 0.08 to 0.14 ppm would be extraordinarily large and argued that the health benefits associated with such standards were nonexistent, or at least very small.[44] Thus a benefit-cost framework would call for a standard in the range of 0.16 to 0.20 ppm.

The EPA made its case by finding that the Clean Air Act Amendments of 1970 specifically prohibited it from using a benefit-cost framework; the agency was instructed to protect the health of the population, including (by implication) the most sensitive members. It sought to estimate a

41. Memorandum, David G. Hawkins, EPA assistant administrator for air and waste management, to Douglas Castle, EPA administrator, "Proposed Revisions to the Existing National Ambient Air Quality Standard for Photochemical Oxidants" (circa 1974), p. 4.

42. Mary W. Wagner and Lanny M. Deal, *Maps Depicting Nonattainment Areas Pursuant to Section 107 of the Clean Air Act* (U.S. Environmental Protection Agency, April 1980), p. viii.

43. Council on Wage and Price Stability, "Environmental Protection Agency's Proposed Revisions to the National Ambient Air Quality Standard for Photochemical Oxidants."

44. Ibid.

threshold at which health effects occurred by asking health experts for their subjective probabilities of the occurrence of various health effects for a range of concentrations. The EPA first asserted that it had used these judgments in setting the standard and then denied that they had played a role.[45] The experts were concerned about too great a reliance being placed on these data, since the encoding procedure had been casual in a number of cases.[46]

Amid intense pressure from environmentalists, administration economists, and business, the EPA set the standard at 0.12 ppm. The agency had loosened the standard from 0.08 ppm and measured only ozone but would loosen it no further. As might have been predicted, the EPA was immediately sued by both sides, one arguing that the standard had been lowered too much and the other that it was still too stringent.

Given this review of the case and the description of the EPA's decision, the eight decision frameworks can be applied and compared with the EPA's decision. The market regulation framework makes no sense for air pollutants. Oxidants are due to millions of individual sources, with no one source being sufficiently important to make a noticeable contribution. No one motorist is motivated to lower his fuel economy and the performance of his car in order to reduce emissions. Yet the vast majority of people agree that emissions should be lowered. This is not a problem that the market can handle, at least not without government intervention to set up effluent fees or marketable discharge rights.

The EPA set its standards under a no-risk framework, but this is a case where "no-risk" has no direct interpretation. Probably no standard within the range of 0.08 to 0.20 ppm could be said to be absolutely protective of the most sensitive member of the population; certainly there is no assurance that 0.12 ppm is as protective as 0.08 ppm. In formulating the standard the EPA must have given some consideration to factors other than risk to health; if not, why would it have relaxed the standard without evidence that 0.12 ppm was safe?

Risk-risk analysis is not applicable.

The Council on Wage and Price Stability argued against the 0.10 ppm proposed standard on the grounds that the cost of curtailing each adverse

45. "Photochemical Oxidants: Proposed Revisions to the National Ambient Air Quality Standard," Federal Register, vol. 43 (June 22, 1978), p. 26966; and "Revisions to the National Ambient Air Quality Standards for Photochemical Oxidants," ibid., vol. 44 (February 8, 1979), p. 8212.

46. Marraro, "The Revision of the Photochemical Oxidant (Ozone) Standard."

health effect would be extraordinarily large, presumably much larger than it would cost to lower such health effects in other parts of the EPA's program.[47] A crude look at the cost-effectiveness framework would indicate that the EPA's oxidant standard is too stringent. Comparing the cost of preventing an adverse health effect under the oxidant and toxic substances standards shows that the former is not cost-effective. Cost-effectiveness would presumably shift attention from oxidants to toxic substances in the environment, especially pesticides and the disposal of toxic wastes.

The council further argued that a benefit-cost framework would call for a standard in the 0.16 to 0.20 ppm range. Although estimates of both costs and benefits are subject to major uncertainty, the council's conclusion is probably correct because costs of control increase rapidly within this range while benefits seem tenuous.

In retrospect the direction of the EPA's revision of the oxidant standard seems obvious. The laboratory and epidemiological studies conducted since 1971 failed to confirm the fears associated with promulgating the first standard. Since many additional cities began to experience problems with photochemical oxidants during this period and the costs of control were recognized to be extremely high, the EPA proposed a token relaxation of the standard (from 0.08 to 0.10 ppm) but was forced to go further. The EPA's analysis of health effects was unsatisfactory, with the agency grasping for straws by using hastily done, inherently suspicious techniques. The no-risk statute enabled the EPA to resist a more significant loosening of the standard, however. Clearly the EPA took account of the costs of meeting various standards but stopped far short of using a benefit-cost framework, or even a cost-effectiveness framework.

Other Air Pollutants

The health effects from photochemical oxidants are of more recent concern than those from suspended particles and sulfur oxides. The literature takes two approaches to identifying the health effects of air pollution from these sources. The first consists of analyses of air pollution episodes such as occurred in London in 1952 when more than 4,000 excess deaths resulted from a prolonged inversion.[48] The second consists of analyses of

47. COWPS, "Environmental Protection Agency's Proposed Revisions to the National Ambient Air Quality Standard for Photochemical Oxidants."
48. A. E. Martin, "Mortality and Morbidity Statistics and Air Pollution," p. 969.

workers or others who were exposed to much higher levels than are experienced by the average public. Both sets of research demonstrate that very high levels of air pollution can lead to excess morbidity and mortality. Neither set, however, is relevant at levels of ambient air quality now typical in U.S. cities; both suggest that society ought to avoid severe episodes and high occupational exposure but do not address the usual levels of air quality.

Estimating the health implications of long-term exposure to lower levels of pollution requires one of two approaches. If the physiological mechanisms by which air pollutants damage health are known, the effects of exposures of laboratory animals at high concentrations may be sufficient to calibrate the functions and provide quantitative estimates of the effects on humans at lower concentrations. Unfortunately little is known of the mechanisms. The other approach consists of epidemiological studies of people exposed to lower levels of air pollution in an attempt to isolate the more subtle effects of exposure to these lower concentrations.

Until more is learned about the physiological mechanisms (from laboratory studies with lower animals and human volunteers or from analysis of natural experiments such as air pollution episodes), there is no alternative to the epidemiological studies. Unfortunately these studies are fraught with controversy because the observed association between pollution and health might be spurious due to some unobserved factors that cause both the air pollution and ill health. A more subtle consequence of possible spurious correlation is that the estimated association might be biased.

These difficulties have been recognized since the 1930s,[49] but a full-scale debate has begun in the last several years regarding the work of Lave and Seskin.[50] Their finding that sulfur oxides and suspended particle levels in most major U.S. cities are consistently and significantly associated with increases in the mortality rate led them to conclude that there is a cause and effect relationship and that abating air pollution would lead to important reductions in the mortality rate (and hence improvements in life expectancy). A series of critics have charged that the results were due in whole or in part to the poor quality of data used in the analysis and to

49. For attempts to control statistically by introducing a population density variable see Lave and Seskin, *Air Pollution and Human Health,* pp. 7–9; Lester B. Lave and Eugene P. Seskin, "Epidemiology, Causality, and Public Policy," p. 179; and P. Stocks, "Recent Epidemiological Studies of Lung Cancer Mortality, Cigarette Smoking, and Air Pollution, with Discussion of a New Hypothesis of Causation," p. 595.

50. Lave and Seskin, *Air Pollution and Human Health.*

the omission of important variables, all of which led to a spurious correlation.[51]

The EPA must review the sulfur oxides standard in 1981 and will do so in the midst of intense controversy over the quality of available research and its interpretation. The EPA's statute will prevent any significant erosion of the current standard, as it did for oxidants, but sulfur oxides differ from oxidants in that a cost-effectiveness or benefit-cost analysis would show that stringent abatement was justified if the estimates of health effects were accepted.[52] Whether one looks at the laboratory evidence or the epidemiological studies, a stronger case for the adverse health effects of sulfur oxides can be made than for oxidants. It appears, however, that the EPA has failed to recognize this distinction and might even reduce the sulfur oxide standard more than the oxidant standard because of industry pressure.

Two gases emitted into the atmosphere that have no short-term health effects but may have devastating effects on climate in the long term are fluorocarbons and carbon dioxide. Fluorocarbons are used as refrigerants and pressurizing gases for spray products. They are extremely stable chemicals that can migrate to the stratosphere, where they reduce ozone, thus increasing the amount of infrared solar radiation reaching the earth's surface. This would be estimated to increase the skin cancer risk for humans, to affect commercial crops, and to affect the ecosystem generally.[53] Although the effects cannot be analyzed in any detail, it is evident that they could be serious. In 1978 the Consumer Product Safety Commission, the Food and Drug Administration, and the EPA banned the use of fluorocarbons in spray cans. Since alternative gases could be used as propellants in consumer products, banning the use of fluorocarbons for this purpose costs very little. Thus analysis showed that a large potential hazard could be reduced with little cost by removing fluorocarbons. The

51. See W. W. Holland and others, "Health Effects of Particulate Pollution: Reappraising the Evidence," pp. 527–659; F. W. Lipfert, "Differential Mortality and the Environment: The Challenge of Multicollinearity in Cross-Sectional Studies," pp. 367–400; T. D. Crocker and others, *Methods of Assessing Air Pollution Control Benefits*, pt. 1: *Experiments in the Economics of Air Pollution Epidemiology;* National Academy of Sciences, *Sulfur Oxides;* and L. A. Thibodeau, R. B. Reed, and Y. M. M. Bishop, "Air Pollution and Human Health: A Review and Reanalysis," pp. 165–83.

52. Lester B. Lave, "The Economics of Sulfur Dioxide Abatement," in Crandall and Lave, eds., *The Scientific Basis of Health and Safety Regulation.*

53. National Academy of Sciences, *Protection Against Depletion of Stratospheric Ozone by Chlorofluorocarbons*, pp. 5–7.

outcome was evident despite the inability to quantify effects with precision.

Increases in atmospheric carbon dioxide result from burning fossil fuels and from clearing forests. Carbon dioxide acts to trap heat being radiated into space, warming the atmosphere, and consequently the surface of the earth. This is commonly known as the greenhouse effect. Given a continuation of the rapid growth in the burning of fossil fuels, a doubling of atmospheric carbon dioxide during the first half of the next century was predicted, with increases in temperature that would average 5 degrees centigrade at the poles and smaller amounts at the equator.[54] Associated with such large changes in temperature are changes in precipitation, wind patterns, and ocean currents, causing the eventual melting of polar ice. Thus the consequences of a substantial increase in atmospheric carbon dioxide are awesome. Neither the time required for a doubling of atmospheric carbon dioxide nor the temperature effects of such a doubling can be predicted with confidence. Furthermore, fossil fuels are so attractive as sources of energy that their use will continue to grow unless very serious consequences can be proved. Sufficient coal, oil shale, and heavy oil exist to multiply atmospheric concentrations of carbon dioxide many times. This is precisely a case where careful analysis can be used to evaluate the seriousness of the potential problem and to formulate solutions. No framework less comprehensive than benefit-cost analysis is likely to prove satisfactory because of the diverse effects, which encompass health, endangered species, equity, and future problems versus current benefits.

Water Pollution

Estimating the costs of water pollution control is comparable to estimating the costs for air pollution control. Uncertainties concern the speed with which controls and discoveries of new control technologies can be introduced. The EPA has produced cost estimates for both air and water pollution.[55]

In contrast to air pollution the estimated health benefits of reduced water pollution are small since central water treatment filters out virtually all the pollutants. Health effects can be large for people drawing water

54. U.S. Department of Energy, *Carbon Dioxide Effects Research and Assessment Program: Workshop on Environmental and Societal Consequences of a Possible CO-Induced Climate Change,* pp. 1–79.

55. EPA, *The Costs of Clean Air;* and EPA, *The Costs of Clean Air and Water.*

directly from a river or a well or being supplied with water from a system too small to have central treatment. The major categories of benefits of reduced water pollution are recreation (due to reduced use of polluted water) and aesthetics (due to the odors or general appearance of polluted waters). These two categories are perhaps the most difficult to measure; current estimates indicate that relatively little benefit would be realized by further abatement of water pollution.[56]

The benefits of water pollution abatement have been researched and analyzed much less than those of air pollution abatement. Cost estimates indicate that abating water pollution will be extraordinarily expensive.[57] While better estimates of benefits will serve to sharpen policy analysis and will result in more confident conclusions, it seems inescapable that stringent abatement of water pollution would lead to costs greatly in excess of benefits. Thus society should go slower than is mandated in the 1972 Water Quality Act. Furthermore, attention should be focused on emissions of pollutants that are not easily trapped in treatment facilities, on treatment procedures, and on those people receiving untreated water.

In spite of the difficulties in getting estimates of benefits or costs in which one can have confidence, the quantitative analyses have contributed both to understanding the issues and to policy formulation. They have served to rule out some proposed policies as either insufficiently or overly stringent; narrowed the set of pollutants that are of primary concern; and served to give a crude priority ordering among issues, pollutants, and geographical areas. The lesson is that even though a formal benefit-cost analysis in which one could have confidence was not possible, quantitative analysis was used to gain insights and to provide policy advice. Some early analysts pushed through formal benefit-cost analyses, making assumptions as necessary.[58] Both at the time and subsequently these analyses have been of limited utility. Ackerman and associates illustrate how a more sensitive treatment of the problems has much to contribute.[59]

56. A. Myrick Freeman III, "The Benefits of Air and Water Pollution Control: A Review and Synthesis of Recent Estimates, pp. 132–74; and Leonard P. Gianessi and Henry M. Peskin, The Distribution of the Costs of Federal Water Pollution Control Policy," pp. 85–102.

57. Peskin and Seskin, eds., *Cost Benefit Analysis and Water Pollution Policy.*

58. Larry B. Barrett and Thomas E. Waddell, *Cost of Air Pollution Damage: A Status Report.*

59. Bruce A. Ackerman and others, *The Uncertain Search for Environmental Quality.*

Pushing the more rigorous quantitative analysis when the data are inadequate accomplishes little, but the range of techniques permits the selection of methods of lesser power whose results are worthy of confidence.

Other Toxic Substances

Many other toxic substances are in the environment, and humans are exposed to them through water or food. Examples include mercury; polychlorinated biphenyls (PCBs); and kepone in fish, lead in paint, pesticide residuals in food, and radionuclides in water and food generally. In some cases the EPA or Food and Drug Administration have performed rough analyses that are unworthy of much confidence; other analyses have been helpful. Three cases of interest are the pesticide chlorobenzilate, exposure of the general population to coke oven emissions, and exposure of the general population to benzene. While there are important uncertainties, these cases demonstrate that analysis can be done and can be helpful in arriving at regulatory decisions.

The most care and attention has been given to the effects of ionizing radiation. Radionuclides escaping to the environment have been identified and measured with some care.[60] Exposures to these radioactive substances, both directly and indirectly through food, have been estimated, with care taken to identify the various types of radiation, target organs, and biological effectiveness of each type of radiation for each organ.[61] The reconcentration of radionuclides in the food chain complicates the analysis.

Estimating the health effects of low-level exposure to ionizing radiation is similar to inferring the effects of low-level exposure to any toxic substance. Acute effects at high doses are known for laboratory animals, but less precisely for humans. Chronic effects due to somewhat lower doses are known in less detail.[62] The doses of ionizing radiation received by the general population, however, or even by people occupationally exposed to radiation, are so low that no direct evidence of effect can be

---

60. Ronald J. Marnicio, "An Examination of the Application of Quantitative Risk Analysis to Ionizing Radiation as Done by the Environmental Protection Agency for 40 CFR Part 190."

61. National Academy of Sciences, *The Effects on Populations of Exposure to Low Levels of Ionizing Radiation.*

62. Thomas K. Mancuso, Alice Stewart, and George Kneale, "Radiation Exposures of Hanford Workers Dying from Cancer and Other Causes," pp. 369–85.

found.[63] Instead, scientists must extrapolate from effects observed at higher doses. There is evidence that a linear dose-response relationship is approximately correct for radiation, although there is intense controversy over whether a best estimate would be that effects are lower than predicted by the linear model at low doses.[64] Radiation is simpler than toxic chemicals to analyze because there is a single type of direct effect (ionized atoms); toxic substances and their metabolites have a host of effects on different organs.

The resources devoted to learning the effects of radiation and then estimating low-level effects are large, especially in comparison with the resources devoted to any other environmental insult. The analyses of radiation present an archetype of how quantitative analyses such as cost-effectiveness and benefit-cost can be done, of the uncertainties, and of how the analysis can be used in setting standards.

Vast experience has been accumulated in estimating the risks of environmental exposures to toxic substances. Since some of the statutes have required frameworks akin to benefit-cost analysis, the difficulties of estimating dose-response relationships have been faced along with attempts to estimate costs and benefits. Where Congress has required a no-risk framework, the impossibility of setting such a standard within an industrial society has generated needless controversy. Although uncertainties remain, it is possible to estimate the risks of toxic substances in the environment and the application of the more general decision frameworks helps improve regulatory decisions.

Health

As the costs of medical care have escalated and the government has assumed a larger role in financing them, pressures for evaluating the efficacy of various preventive and therapeutic procedures have increased. Attempting to infer whether a particular action has a particular effect is exceedingly difficult without the ability to experiment. Confounding factors are so important as to raise questions about the ability to infer causation or to estimate the magnitude of the response.[65] While this problem is

63. NAS, *The Effects on Populations of Exposure to Low Levels of Ionizing Radiation*.

64. Ibid., pp. 4, 25.

65. "Identification, Classification and Regulation of Potential Occupational Carcinogens," *Federal Register*, vol. 45 (January 22, 1980), pp. 5038–53; and

common to many areas, ethical reasons for not giving each patient less than the best care make it ubiquitous in health. A randomized clinical trial, where patients are randomly assigned among two or more competing treatments, is possible only when the participating physicians, study sponsors, and the medical community at large feel that the competing treatments promise approximately the same benefit to each patient. Thus if physicians are convinced that one treatment dominates, they are precluded from testing their belief and from estimating the magnitude of the benefit. This means that the vast majority of medical practices have never been tested and will never be tested, even though on the basis of previous experience there is good reason to suspect that a large proportion are not efficacious or are even harmful.[66]

The Americans' cultural heritage is typified by films from the 1930s in which any medical problem could be cured if only the victim could get the assistance of the Mayo Clinic. This general belief is reinforced by the miracles of medical intervention; broken bones are mended, eyesight corrected, infection cured, and hearts transplanted. Rates of morbidity and mortality, however, have little relationship to the quality and quantity of personal health services. Life expectancy is not greatest in the country with the most advanced biomedical research or even in the country with the greatest per capita expenditures on medical care. Instead, a growing part of the health care community has come to conclude that general health, morbidity rates, and life expectancy are influenced more by genetic heritage, exercise habits, diet, and such environmental factors as stress than by personal health services.[67] While this general skepticism about the value of personal health services is of no direct relevance in evaluating a particular program, it does condition evaluation in two ways. The first is

---

Brian McMahon, T. Puch, and Johannes Ipsen, *Epidemiologic Methods* (Little, Brown, 1960).

66. A. L. Cochrane, *Effectiveness and Efficiency: Random Reflections on Health Services* (United Kingdom: Nuffield Provincial Hospitals Trust, 1972); John P. Bunker, Benjamin A. Barnes, and Frederick Mosteller, eds., *Costs, Risks, and Benefits of Surgery;* and John E. Wennberg, John P. Bunker, and Benjamin Barnes, "The Need for Assessing the Outcome of Common Medical Practices," pp. 277–96.

67. Lave and Seskin, *Air Pollution and Human Health,* p. 9; Belloc, "Relationship of Health Practices and Mortality," pp. 67–81; Nedra B. Belloc and Lester Breslow, "Relationship of Physical Health Status and Health Practices," pp. 409–21; Lester Breslow and James E. Enstrom, "The Persistence of Health Habits and Their Relationship to Mortality," pp. 469–83; and Ernst L. Wynder, "The Dietary Environment and Cancer," pp. 385–91.

a general skepticism about the merit of "miracle drugs" or "miracle treatments." These are likely to have more side effects than anticipated and to prove less effective than their discoverers claim. Indeed, the major benefit is likely to come from a placebo effect. The second is a heightened responsibility to carry out evaluations, even where a new technique appears to be efficacious on the basis of a small number of case studies.

With the nationalization of health services after World War II, Great Britain put stringent budget limitations on health services.[68] This caused the National Health Service to resist many new expensive or unproved techniques in favor of expanding simple, proved ones. Budget pressures also caused the administration of randomized clinical trials in order to ensure that an expensive new technique was effective before introducing it. A. L. Cochrane cites the value of clinical trials, in spite of the cost and time required, arguing that purely observational data, such as case studies, offer little information because of the confounding factors.[69] Randomized clinical trials have been done all over the world.[70] They have provided quantitative estimates of the efficacy of the treatment studied, including the costs and quantitative degree of improvement. Going from these data to a benefit-cost analysis is straightforward, although the additional assumptions are certain to add controversy.

Bunker and associates and Wennberg and associates examine the efficacy of past and present surgical procedures.[71] Their studies, unlike Cochrane's, focus on the qualitative question of whether the surgical procedure helps. While one must grant that the focus is on unfortunate procedures, the reader carries away a general sense of skepticism about surgical procedures in general. Several chapters are devoted to a series of disease treatments that do prove effective, although at vast differences in the cost per additional year of life expectancy. For example, Bendixen describes a range of cases involving intensive care, from barbiturate overdose where life expectancy is prolonged at $84 a year to hepatorenal failure in chronic

68. Gwyn Bevan and others, *Health Care: Priorities and Management*, pp. 6, 12–20.

69. Cochrane, *Effectiveness and Efficiency*, pp. 20–25.

70. See reviews in ibid.; David L. Sackett, "Screening for Early Detection of Disease to What Purpose?" p. 51; Wennberg, Bunker, and Barnes, "The Need for Assessing the Outcome of Common Medical Practices"; and Bunker, Barnes, and Mosteller, eds., *Costs, Risks, and Benefits of Surgery*.

71. Bunker, Barnes, and Mosteller, eds., *Costs, Risks, and Benefits of Surgery;* and Wennberg, Bunker, and Barnes, "The Need for Assessing the Outcome of Common Medical Practices."

alcoholics where life expectancy is prolonged at a cost of $180,000 a year.[72] The two extremes in Bendixen's study are defined by patients with drug abuse; both crises result from self-inflicted damage. The assumed increase in life expectancy for the barbiturate overdose patient may be too high if the individual is determined to attempt suicide again.

A major goal of the studies of Bunker and associates is to remove the mystery from the use of quantitative evaluation and decision techniques in medical care. They show that these techniques are extremely helpful and not terribly difficult to apply. Thus there is no doubt that quantitative evaluation techniques can be and are being applied to personal health services. Ethical considerations mean that some well-established techniques will never be evaluated and that some new techniques are likely to be adopted without evaluation. There are no good ethical or financial reasons, however, for not evaluating the vast majority of new treatments. Several reviews of the literature using these quantitative techniques show an increasing number of studies are now being done and published.[73]

Preventive health measures have a long history of formal evaluation. Yet if anything, they are more difficult to evaluate than therapeutic services. There is a large literature evaluating inoculations, screening, and asymptomatic examinations.[74] In addition, a literature is accumulating on attempts to change health habits and to educate people about how to achieve better health.[75]

Much of the literature in the past half-decade goes beyond the usual

72. Henrik H. Bendixen, "The Cost of Intensive Care," in Bunker, Barnes, and Mosteller, *Costs, Risks, and Benefits of Surgery,* pp. 377–79. According to Bendixen, barbiturate overdose occurs predominately in young adults; nineteen out of twenty of these patients survive and about four days of hospitalization are required at a total cost of $2,400. The high survival rate and youth of the patients mean that life expectancy is being prolonged at a cost of only about $84 a year. However, only one alcoholic in five with hepatorenal failure survives, and those that do are expected to live only one year; hospitalization of about thirty days is required at a total cost of $36,000. In sharp contrast to the individuals with barbiturate overdose, life expectancy for these alcoholics is prolonged at a cost of about $180,000 a year.

73. See, for example, Elizabeth M. Clark and Andrew J. Van Horn, *Risk-Benefit Analysis and Public Policy: A Bibliography;* and U.S. Office of Technology Assessment, *The Implications of Cost-Effectiveness Analysis of Medical Technology,* Background Paper 1: *Methodological Issues and Literature Review.*

74. For a survey of the literature see Lester B. Lave and others, "Economic Impact of Preventive Medicine."

75. Belloc, "Relationship of Health Practices and Mortality"; Belloc and Breslow, "Relationship of Physical Health Status and Health Practices"; and Breslow and Enstrom, "Persistence of Health Habits and Their Relationship to Mortality."

evaluation of efficacy by presenting a benefit-cost analysis or at least estimates of the cost of prolonging life or avoiding an untoward event. Many of the analyses are self-serving in the sense that the qualitative outcome was known in advance; the benefit-cost analysis resulted from an attempt to buttress a position. Thus quantitative analysis has been used to argue that preventive care, inoculations, or various research programs generally ought to receive more resources.[76] The use of quantitative analysis is rare in many programs for children where more is spent than would be justified by a benefit-cost analysis (a notable exception is screening for phenylketonuria).[77]

Transport Safety

Many of the difficulties in analyzing health services also arise in analyzing accidents. Identifying the immedate and contributory causes of each is controversial, as is attempting to infer what actions might prevent or reduce adverse health consequences. A major simplification for accidents is the ability to link each with the place of occurrence, such as a highway; rarely can chronic disease be linked to an individual activity, location, or exposure. Both accidents and chronic disease, however, have multiple, interacting causes. Even if they are not the immediate cause, the use of psychoactive drugs, fatigue, negligence, and ignorance contribute to accidents. It is tempting to seek easy solutions by changing the design or construction of some product, such as the automobile, rather than by attempting to deal with the more important factors of personal behavior. Vehicle design or mechanical failures are responsible for only a small fraction of accidents; most are caused by the behavior of the occupant.[78]

76. Lester Lave and others, "Economic Impact of Preventive Medicine," pp. 688–98; Barbara S. Cooper and Dorothy P. Rice, "The Economic Cost of Illness Revisited," pp. 21–36; D. P. Rice and T. A. Hodgson, "Social and Economic Implications of Cancer in the United States," pp. 56–100; and Dorothy P. Rice, Jacob I. Feldman, and Kerr L. White, "The Current Burden of Illness in the United States," pp. 19–29.

77. Neil A. Holtzman, Allen G. Meek, and E. David Mellits, "Neonatal Screening for Phenylketonuria," pt. 1: "Effectiveness," pp. 667–70; and Barbara Starfield and Neil A. Holtzman, "A Comparison of Effectiveness of Screening for Phenylketonuria in the United States, United Kingdom, and Ireland," pp. 118–21.

78. U.S. Office of Technology Assessment, *Technology Assessment of Changes in the Future Use and Characteristics of the Automobile Transportation System*, vol. 2: *Technical Report*, chap. 10.

The number of serious accidents and deaths occurring in transportation is widely disseminated information.[79] Individual accidents, especially those involving the deaths of more than one person, are much publicized. Publicity about specific accidents, especially air crashes, combines with annual statistics to create public pressure for regulatory actions to make transportation safer. The safety of each of the major modes of transportation is regulated by a specific agency charged with improving safety. Two agencies, the Federal Aviation Administration (FAA) and the National Highway Traffic Safety Administration (NHTSA), have been especially active in preparing quantitative analyses of new designs, safety features, and operating procedures that would enhance safety. Each agency prepares an analysis of the extent to which risks would be lowered and property damage and injury averted, as well as the estimated costs of a proposed new regulation. While controversy is inevitable, these two agencies have firmly established the tradition of analyzing proposed regulations.

Air Transport

In 1978 the FAA issued a report on an analysis of frangible approach lighting systems at U.S. airports.[80] The report identifies the principal benefit of these easily broken lighting poles to be an enhancement of safety when the pole is struck by an aircraft. Secondary benefits include lower maintenance and less energy use.

Potential accident reduction is estimated by tabulating recent experience by air carriers and general aviation to determine which accidents were due to collision with a rigid light pole. Health outcomes are tabulated in categories of death and serious or minor injury. The value to society of preventing injury was taken from an analysis of actual settlements, $300,000 for death, $45,000 for serious injury, and $6,000 for minor injury. The dollar values for the two injury categories, particularly serious injury, seem underestimated, since some injuries involve long hospitalizations and permanent disability. Damage to aircraft is estimated on the basis of replacing the aircraft with a comparable used one or repairing the damage. Maintenance savings are estimated via the reduction

79. National Safety Council, *Accident Facts, 1980 Edition*, pp. 40–71.
80. U.S. Federal Aviation Administration, *Installation Criteria for the Approach Lighting System Improvement Plan (ALSIP)*.

in man-hours at the current wage rates. Energy savings are valued at $0.05 per kilowatt-hour.

The number of accidents caused or aggravated by collision with lighting standards was divided by the total number of operations during this period to get the average risk per operation. The total damage sustained in the accidents, injury plus aircraft damage, was tabulated and divided by the number of operations to get the average loss per operation due to collision with rigid light standards.

The benefits of various proposals are estimated by multiplying the expected number of operations at these airports by the cost reduction due to safe operations. These present discounted costs are $14.59 per operation for air carriers and 22 cents per operation for general aviation. The FAA reported that 397 lighting systems are candidates for replacement at a total cost of $77.7 million. Of these, 272 with a total cost of $48.4 million have benefits greater than costs.

The report is technically well done in carrying out the benefit-cost analysis, and the FAA is to be praised for attempting an analysis for each candidate runway rather than attempting to compare the total benefits of the program with its total costs. The report, however, does not go so far as to rank candidate runways by their benefit-cost ratio in order to determine where the FAA ought to concentrate its initial efforts. One might quarrel with the parameter values used to estimate the social cost of injury, but there is a reasonable basis for the estimated parameters. A major weakness is the estimated reduction in accidents stemming from frangible lighting systems, but it is difficult to imagine how better estimates could be achieved from available data. The report is to be commended, but it could have been improved by explicit discussion of the estimates; the current report puts the burden on the reader to infer in what ways the estimates were imprecise.

The eight decision frameworks can be applied to setting a standard for frangible light poles. Market regulation would call for the FAA to present this analysis to airport managers and allow them to make their own decisions. The FAA is currently responsible for air safety, and a change in legislation might be required to allow airports to make their own decisions. A no-risk framework would call for frangible standards at all airports, with a large increase in expenditures. While the FAA could probably fund this program, it could not fund the implementation of all programs that would reduce risk in commercial and civil aviation. The risk-risk (indirect) framework could be applied here, since constructing and erecting the new light poles would be expected to result in occupational injuries and disease. Although it is conceptually possible to estimate the increase in occupational injuries, the increase is likely to be small. Technology-based standards would lead the FAA to replace all light poles; as with the no-risk framework, the FAA would be unable to obtain sufficient funds to implement best available technology throughout aviation. Risk-benefit would probably compare the risk per hour of flying with the risk of other activities. Since the risk is somewhat higher, this activity would probably be deemed to need improvement, and so the FAA would be asked to undertake a series of steps to enhance safety, such as frangible lighting standards, presumably without differentiating between large and small airports.

The cost-effectiveness and regulatory budget frameworks would lead to solutions similar to that proposed by the FAA if the FAA budget were at a level that permitted implementation of all standards whose benefits exceeded their costs. The FAA has acted in a disciplined, responsible fashion and both the Department of Transportation and Congress have learned to trust their analyses.

This is a case where applying frameworks other than cost-effectiveness, regulatory budget, and benefit-cost analysis would have led to a less desirable solution. Certainly controversies were associated with the assumed value placed on preventing an accidental death, and with airports that did not receive the new light poles, but the quality of the analysis prevailed.

Auto Safety: Passive Seat Belts

About 50,000 people are killed on highways each year, making highway accidents the most common cause of death of young adults. The NHTSA was established to lower this slaughter. One key part of the solution is to restrain occupants during a crash. Seat belts are extraordinarily effective; it is estimated that the number of fatalities and serious injuries would be lowered 50 percent if all occupants wore three-point belts.[81] In practice only about 14 percent of occupants wear their belts. Thus a highly effective safety device is almost totally useless in practice.

The NHTSA attempted to compel people to buckle up in 1974- and

---

81. R. A. Wilson and C. M. Savage, "Restraint System Effectiveness: A Study of Fatal Accidents"; and Donald F. Huelke and others, *Effectiveness of Current and Future Restraint Systems in Fatal and Serious Injury Automobile Crashes.*

early 1975-model automobiles by requiring an interlock device, which would keep the automobile from being driven unless all occupants had buckled their belts. The combination of mechanical problems and public resentment, however, led Congress to forbid the NHTSA to continue requiring the device. Since 1975 the NHTSA has been searching for a way of protecting occupants without requiring a belt to be buckled or a similar action. This concern resulted in a standard calling for cars to be designed so that front-seat occupants, without having to buckle seat belts or take other protective action, would receive no more than minor injuries if their automobile crashed head-on or at an angle of up to 30 degrees in either direction into a solid barrier at 30 miles per hour.[82] This requirement was scheduled to be phased in from model years 1982 to 1984, beginning with the large cars.

Two current safety systems are capable of meeting the standard. The first is an air bag system, where bags in the steering wheel and dashboard inflate rapidly in case of a collision, holding the occupant in the seat. The other is a passive seat belt that automatically operates without passenger action. Difficulties with air bags include their expense; the lack of protection for side crashes, multiple collisions, or rollovers; danger to young children; premature deployment; and damage from being activated by vandals. The air bags are markedly more expensive than either the current seat belts or passive belts. Air bags are less effective, however, if a lap seat belt is not worn.[83] Their principal advantages are that they allow occupants to be completely unencumbered by belts and permit a bench front seat. Of the two devices, air bags are more expensive, provide less protection, and are most costly to repair after an accident. Passive seat belts have all the disadvantages of seat belts, except that they are automatically activated. Some people object to being confined; the NHTSA estimates that 22 percent of occupants may disable their passive belts in order to avoid being confined.[84]

A major issue is the extent to which people are or should be capable of making their own safety decisions. Public and government reaction has been ambiguous. By requiring safety equipment for automobiles, the

82. 49 C.F.R. 571.

83. Huelke and O'Day, "The National Highway Traffic Safety Administration Passive Restraint System: A Scientist's Viewpoint," in Crandall and Lave, eds., *The Scientific Basis of Health and Safety Regulations.*

84. Carol Stowell and Joseph Bryant, *Safety Belt Usage: Survey of Cars in the Traffic Population,* p. 21.

NHTSA is assuming that buyers are not able to make correct decisions concerning their own safety. But failing to require people to wear the required seat belts is an admission either that the regulation could not be enforced or that it should not be made. This schizophrenia about whether people are responsible leads to costly decisions. If people are not responsible, seat belts ought to be required and their wearing should be mandatory. If people are responsible, they can make their own decisions about wearing seat belts, and safety equipment should not be required.

Major controversy erupted between the Department of Transportation and the automobile companies about the number of lives that would be saved by air bags or passive belts. It was first estimated that 25,000 people would be saved each year, then 10,500, and then 9,000.[85] The automobile companies were more skeptical, although they gradually raised their estimates over time. A series of social experiments has reduced the range of uncertainty. A fleet of General Motors cars was equipped with air bags and then studied for crash protection. Volkswagen equipped some cars with passive belts and these cars have been studied. Sufficient experience has been accumulated to result in general agreement about the number of fatalities (6,300 to 9,000 a year) and serious injuries (about 41,000 a year) that would be averted by air bags, air bags and lap belts, or passive belts (that have not been disconnected).

Quantitative analysis has not resolved the issue of whether air bags, passive seat belts, or the wearing of standard belts should be required, but it has provided estimates of the benefits stemming from each of these policies and of the costs of each. The ultimate decision requires much more than quantitative analysis. It is evident, however, that the analysis has managed to rule out many proposed solutions and clarify the implications of others.

The eight decision frameworks can be applied to passive seat belts. Market regulation would call for offering these devices as optional features, disseminating information to consumers, and letting them make their own decisions. Since only a small proportion of buyers elected either the passive seat belts or air bags in available models, it seems likely that few buyers would elect them in the future. The result would be little or no decrease in the number of severe or fatal highway accidents. Society appears to have made a decision that the number of highway deaths and

85. Huelke and O'Day, "The National Highway Traffic Safety Administration Passive Restraint System."

severe injuries is too large to be tolerated. Thus the market solution is not recognized as commensurate with social goals. But the failure of automobile occupants to fasten their current seat belts, and the fact that perhaps one-fourth of owners of automobiles with passive seat belts disconnect them, means that the new standard will be less than totally effective in achieving social goals. Even though the market solution is not socially acceptable, it cannot be dismissed lightly.

The no-risk framework would require the air bags in combination with lap seat belts, since this combination appears to be most effective. But injuries could be reduced even more effectively by lowering speed limits, prohibiting people from driving while drunk or fatigued, and taking away the licenses of accident-prone drivers. This solution has not been attempted.

The risk-risk framework adds little, since the increase in occupational injuries from making the passive restraint devices would be small.

Technology-based standards would require these devices as best available technology. There are a host of other devices that would add to safety dramatically, including designing an automobile to be crash resistant, but these would increase the cost of an automobile. The NHTSA has not required best available technology.

One interpretation of risk-benefit analysis is that society should equalize risk per hour of activity. If so, the framework would call for the passive restraints on the grounds that riding in an automobile is more dangerous per hour than other activities. Indeed, it would presumably call for the redesign of the automobile until it was as safe as other activities, even though this would increase the price of a car to the point of denying it to many current owners.

Cost-effectiveness analysis would call for passive restraints. To be exact, it would call for passive belts since they are more cost-effective than air bags. As long as they are not disconnected, they save lives at approximately the cost of other NHTSA regulations. This analysis would probably not take account of consumer preferences and might not consider the number of devices that would be disconnected. The regulatory budget would probably lead to the same outcome as cost-effectiveness analysis, with the same difficulties.

A benefit-cost analysis would probably also lead to requiring the passive restraints. The analysis should account for the number of devices that would be disconnected, an action that would lower benefits. More difficult would be considering people's feelings about being required to pay for and use these devices when they desired current seat belts or no encumbrance. Society can desire a reduction in highway deaths but reject a safety device—for example, the interlock. Society must decide whether the reduction in death and serious injuries from automobile accidents justifies the increased price of cars, requiring people to accept air bags or passive belts, and denying ownership to those who cannot afford the increase in vehicle cost. While benefit-cost analysis does not weigh all these factors into summary numbers, it does stress consideration of all these effects.

Consumer Products

The Consumer Product Safety Commission was created to regulate accident and disease risks from products purchased and used by consumers.[86] Recognizing that some degree of risk was inherent in all products, Congress created a statute that requires the CPSC to balance risks and benefits in setting standards. Thus analyses have been done using a risk-benefit framework, with only rough attempts to quantify costs and benefits, monetize them, and complete a benefit-cost analysis.

The requirement for analysis and balancing did not prevent the agency from proposing an ill-advised standard for swimming pool slides, but it did enable the manufacturer to get the standard set aside.[87] These analyses helped persuade manufacturers of cribs to alter the spacing of their bars so that an infant's head could not be trapped. Nothing as formal as benefit-cost analysis is needed to make the case for cribs since the costs of altering their design is virtually zero; the only issue is whether widely spaced bars present enough of a risk that redesign is required. Crib design is probably a case where market regulation would be sufficient. Giving the public information about the threat of widely spaced bars could be expected to shift purchases. Even those who do not care about the risk would eventually be protected because better-informed consumers, refusing to purchase unsafe cribs, would thus reduce the market for them

86. Richard A. Merrill, "Federal Regulation of Cancer-Causing Chemicals," chap. 3: "CPSC Regulation of Consumer Products Presenting Chronic Health Hazards," pp. 1–4.

87. Ibid., p. 25.

and profitability to the point where such cribs would no longer be manufactured. In addition, governmental identification of the risk would be a valuable aid for the parents of an infant injured or killed in a poorly designed crib; they could expect to collect damages in a suit against the retailer and manufacturer. This threat of substantial awards would provide even more incentive for manufacturers to change their design.

A set of proposed standards for lawn mower safety is another example of the use of quantitative analysis. The Council on Wage and Price Stability analyzed these standards and challenged them, finding simplistic the CPSC's conclusion that benefits would exceed costs under one set of assumptions. The primary goal of the council's analysis is to examine each of the proposed design changes and to estimate the benefits and costs of each. The analysis shows that some of the changes are cost-effective, while others are absurd. The separation of standards showed that virtually all the increase in consumer safety could be achieved for a small fraction of the cost of the entire package.[88]

To date, few of the CPSC analyses have been of sufficient quality to support good decisions. Despite difficulties in estimating costs and benefits, there is no reason why the analyses could not have been improved, as shown by the council's study. In at least one case, the regulation on flame-resistant children's sleepwear, the rush to solve a problem led to a solution (adding Tris to flammable fabrics) that probably imposed greater risks than were present before the regulation.

Impact Statements: The Misuse of Analysis

Overselling the value of analysis is evident in various types of impact statements required by the president and Congress. To determine the effects of new legislation or agency regulations on some social goal and to ensure that Congress and the agency recognize these effects, the president and Congress have mandated environmental and inflationary impact statements. While the intent of these requirements was noble, there can be little doubt that few beneficial results have followed. The principal effect has been to slow the passage of new legislation, the enactment of agency decisions, and the commencement of private sector projects. Since the

88. Thomas M. Lenard, "Lawn Mower Safety," in James C. Miller III and Bruce Yandle, eds., *Benefit-Cost Analyses of Social Regulation: Case Studies from the Council on Wage and Price Stability.*

requirements for these various impact statements were never defined rigorously nor was their role in decisionmaking specified, their effect has been confined largely to stopping a project until a satisfactory (usually defined by the courts) statement has been prepared.[89] Generally the resulting impact statements are so voluminous that no one considers or even reads them, much less attempts to modify decisions on the basis of their findings. This is surely one of those cases of overload where additional data are not examined and thus have no role in decisionmaking. If some future impact statement is to affect decisionmaking, other than to slow it, the nature of the analysis must be carefully defined, along with the role the resulting information is to have in making decisions. Merely preparing something that is vaguely relevant provides no assurance that it will prove useful. Analyses must be specified carefully and tailored to the needs of decisionmakers. If not, they become millstones about the necks of people trying to make decisions; they contribute nothing and slow the process.

Conclusion

This chapter has presented a series of case studies of analyses performed to support decisions in regulating occupational health and safety, the environment, health, transport safety, and consumer products. Whether the subject is food additives or lawn mowers, the case studies exhibit similar problems: the scientific foundation is virtually always incomplete, quantitative analyses are fraught with uncertainty, equity issues are important, and society's goals are unclear.

There is a scientific foundation for analyzing the risk of exposure to toxic substances and of accident hazards, but the foundation is incomplete and often rudimentary. Insofar as each of the analyses contributed to decisionmaking, and insofar as each had uncertainties, there was a need for handling these uncertainties explicitly. Dealing explicitly with uncertainty is often the most difficult aspect of an analysis.

One possible implication of these problems is that quantitative analysis is impossible, or at least useless. The analyses do provide insights into decisionmaking, however. Although analysis is difficult, it is necessary to impose order on splintered, multifaceted problems. Quantitative analysis

89. Michael S. Baram, "Regulation of Health, Safety and Environmental Quality and the Use of Cost-Benefit Analysis."

can be done in each area and the information developed is needed to improve regulatory decisionmaking.

Analysis is not an end in itself. This has been demonstrated by environmental and inflationary impact statements, which have served mainly to delay implementation of new programs. The difficulties and complexities of these problems underline the need for sensible analysis; at the same time they show how easily the analysis can become useless or pernicious.

CHAPTER SIX

The Benefits and Costs
of Benefit-Cost Analysis

". . . the essential function of scientists is not to tell the regulatory agency what to do, but to define the risks and benefits as objectively as they can and, what is more, make them known to the public. Those are the obligations of the scientists. Don't worry about these legal guys. They write laws and come out with all kinds of things. But if the people know what they're up against and have before them the basis on which conclusions are reached, I think you'll accomplish much more than you will by any legalistic process or by any labeling process."
—R. Hertz, "Public Policy Panels," in Howard H. Hiatt, James D. Watson, and Jay A. Winsten, eds., *Origins of Human Cancer,* 1977

ANY CASE HISTORY of a social decision, such as the attempted ban of saccharin, will reveal the complexities of the decision. Furthermore, a decision has myriad consequences, few of which can be forecast. For example, somewhat tongue in cheek White asserts that an important cause of the French Revolution was the invention of the chimney (since it allowed nobles to live apart from their peasants and to develop a progressively disparate life-style, eventually leading to the excesses of 18th century France).[1]

In the midst of this complexity each regulatory agency must set priorities to correct the worst cases, reduce confusion by providing a clear signal about agency goals and procedures—particularly to decisionmakers not covered by the specific regulations—and influence decisionmakers to move toward accomplishing society's goals. Ad hoc decisions are unlikely to accomplish any of these objectives. Jumping from crisis to crisis may seem responsive but is not the best way to spot important cases early, provide defensible regulations, or generate a model for other decisionmakers. Indeed, by fostering crisis an agency diverts attention from each of these goals.

1. Lynn White, Jr., "Technology Assessment from the Stance of a Medieval Historian," pp. 8–9.

Specific regulations cover only a tiny fraction of decisions concerning health and safety. Were an agency to choose subjects at random, it would be unlikely ever to deal with the most important areas. Were its efforts to apply only to the specific regulations it promulgated, it would have little effect on health and safety. To accomplish the social goals of enhancing health and safety, there is no alternative to a less frenetic, more analytic approach. But it is easy to overstate the contribution of quantitative analysis, which cannot possibly deal with more than one small aspect of a social decision, and that only imprecisely. Thus if the question is whether quantitative analysis should be the only input into a social decision, the answer is clearly no.

It is equally extreme to assert that quantitative analysis can make no useful contribution to the decision. Despite all the aspects such analysis cannot treat and all the uncertainties associated with the aspects it can treat, analysis can help to identify more imaginative alternatives, define the implications of decisions, attain goals at lower cost, identify actions that cannot pass technical muster, and clarify the trade-offs among competing goals.

The major arguments for and against the use of quantitative analysis reflect different ways of approaching a problem. For example, the social problem of air pollution can be seen as an ethical issue: moral people attempt to clean the environment, while evil or lazy people resist them. In political terms the problem consists of groups vying for power and being willing to offer support on one set of issues in return for support on another set. In legal terms the problem is to restore to people their right to clean air, a right that was usurped by industrial polluters. These views and others have been represented in the debate. Each offers insights into the way in which the struggle has progressed and helps explain the positions of various groups, their willingness to compromise on some issues, and their evolution in the face of changing events.

Technical-Economic Approaches

A technical-economic approach to a problem such as pollution is quite different from the moral, political, or legal approaches. For example, benefit-cost analysis attempts to define social goals in terms of maximizing social welfare or minimizing social cost and to implement these social goals as efficiently as possible (least cost and least delay). The more elaborate decision frameworks (risk-benefit, cost-effectiveness, regulatory budget, and benefit-cost) require discovering which pollutants are most harmful and how they can be abated most cheaply. By giving short shrift to equity, politics, and due process they focus on the aspects of the problem that can be quantified, but they neglect large and highly important parts of the world.

The question is not whether quantitative analysis neglects important issues, since it surely does. Rather, the question is whether, or under what conditions, quantitative analysis provides valuable insights. For example, Congress set specific emission standards for automobiles in the Clean Air Act Amendments of 1970. With virtually no data on control costs, air quality, or health effects, Congress mandated a 90 percent reduction in emissions of each pollutant. The legislation fails to recognize that some pollutants are more harmful or more costly to abate than others and that abating emissions carries with it costs in accomplishing other social goals, such as better fuel economy.[2] The amendments were strongly influenced by ethical, legal, and political views, but their authors rejected the technical-economic frameworks. As might be expected, the legislation had solid ethical and political appeal but proved impossible to implement as written; what was implemented was costly, a continuing source of controversy, and subject to numerous delays. One danger of regulations based on ethics and political power is that they may be obsolete before they are implemented due to shifts in public consensus. Thus economic difficulties in the automobile industry in 1980 caused many regulations to be suspended. There is nothing wrong with revising regulatory decisions in the face of new evidence; automobile emission regulations, however, have been revised almost annually in a government-business confrontation that damages institutions and delays achieving clean air.

As demonstrated in the first half of this book, quantitative analysis is necessary at each stage in order to identify the magnitude of human risk, to find the least-cost methods of abatement, and to identify groups at especially high risk.

The strengths of quantitative analysis are that it generates more alternatives, reveals conflicting goals, balances these conflicts, and points to ways to implement the goals at low cost; its weaknesses are the sparse treatment given to equity issues and insensitivity to the political process. The Federal Aviation Administration analysis of frangible lighting standards is one extreme case in which there was no doubt about the cause of

2. Lester B. Lave, "Conflicting Objectives in Regulating the Automobile: The Interdependence of Safety, Emissions and Fuel Economy."

the accidents and only modest doubt about the benefits to be gained; the decision was almost entirely within the agency and not subject to important political pressure. An opposing example is the Food and Drug Administration's decision to ban diethylstilbestrol when great uncertainty remains about the compound's health effects and about ethical issues concerning genital malformations, infertility, and cancer in unborn children. The DES example should not be interpreted to mean that quantitative analysis has no insights to offer; the analysis in chapter 4 is of help in deciding whether to ban DES, although it is not the only important input.

Data Collection and Analysis

Several questions were raised at the beginning of this book. Is quantitative analysis helpful in making social decisions? Are the required data available? The studies reviewed imply that the answer to both questions is a qualified yes. Quantitative analysis is helpful but is only one input to the decision. In many cases it will be a small, relatively unimportant input.

Data are collected only if there is a need. While initial attempts at quantitative analysis may turn up relatively little data, the growing use and importance of such analysis will lead to more data collection. Often, all that is required to get data collection started is a recognition of the pertinent data, which is seldom expensive or time-consuming to collect. The major point is that without data and analysis, we are guessing. When millions of lives and tens of billions of dollars of resources are at stake, guessing is simply not a satisfactory way to formulate public policy.

Social regulation and pure science are antithetical in that both resources and time are limited for the former. The most felicitous framework for regulation is not the most general; the important issues must be raised first and in a way that facilitates decisionmaking. The framework must also assign tasks to the institutions best equipped to undertake them and push aside, politely, the issues of lesser importance. For example, Congress has the authority to set general goals and resolve value conflicts. A framework that allows Congress to shirk these difficult issues and delegate them to a regulatory agency will lead to goals reflecting a narrow constituency rather than society generally, to increased opposition and litigation, and to failure in accomplishing the social goals giving rise to the legislation.

A common misperception is that analysis makes no contribution unless it can resolve all the problems. Rarely are the available data and analysis able to resolve even the most important problems. Significant uncertainties always remain because a crucial parameter is unknown or a question is currently unanswerable. Rather, the analysis must examine the implications of each aspect of uncertainty and attempt to find solutions that dominate their alternatives despite the remaining uncertainties.

Implementing such analyses would require a major shift in personnel and resource allocation within regulatory agencies. One might hope that fewer lawyers would be needed to make judgments on the basis of inadequate evidence, to interpret the fine points of a statute, and to defend the agency in litigation. More analysts would be required to augment current data collection and analysis of regulatory alternatives. Certainly there would have to be some legal interpretation and litigation, but legal judgments would be made on the basis of much better information. Reallocating resources in this way should produce better regulations more clearly in the public interest, thereby helping to mollify those who must pay the cost of a regulation and making legal defense easier.

Case Studies

I have reviewed a small number of studies drawn from a vast literature on quantitative analysis of social policies. This literature demonstrates that quantitative analysis can be done and that it offers insights into social policy regarding such diverse areas as food additives, personal health services, and automobile safety. Indeed, quantitative analysis changes the way one examines each of these areas. This is particularly evident in the general skepticism expressed by Cochrane regarding personal health services.[3] His insistence on evaluation leads to the identification and rejection not only of care that is useless, but what is more important, of care that is pernicious. Without such a rigorous approach, health care is determined by small samples and prejudice. One result is the proliferation of surgical procedures that are harmful.[4]

There are costs to quantitative analysis, however. One cost is bad deci-

3. A. L. Cochrane, *Effectiveness and Efficiency: Random Reflections on Health Services* (United Kingdom: Nuffield Provincial Hospitals Trust, 1972).

4. John P. Bunker, Benjamin A. Barnes, and Frederick Mosteller, eds., *Costs, Risks, and Benefits of Surgery*, pp. 387–95; and John E. Wennberg, John P. Bunker, and Benjamin Barnes, "The Need for Assessing the Outcome of Common Medical Practices," pp. 277–96.

sions resulting from endowing the estimated numbers with too much confidence and tending to ignore unquantified aspects; this cost is the flip side of dismissing analysis as useless. The costs of data collection, analysis, and interpretation must also be considered. For example, Cochrane's randomized clinical trials are exceedingly expensive. The National Health Service of Great Britain could devote all its resources to clinical trials testing accepted procedures rather than to giving care to British residents. While asserting the benefit of analysis, one must temper one's enthusiasm with a qualification concerning how much of the total resources should be devoted to analysis. I cannot pretend to give firm answers, but even slightly better data and analysis would have saved society billions of dollars and thousands of lives in medical care or air pollution abatement. Clearly society has spent too little on quantitative analysis in the past.

Chapters 4 and 5 demonstrate that data are routinely available or could be collected inexpensively to do quantitative analyses in many areas of social policy. Analyses have provided, and are likely to continue to provide, important insights for legislation and regulatory policy. Thus I find no insurmountable obstacles to the application of these techniques and recommend that the president and Congress mandate one or the other of the regulatory frameworks relying on quantitative analysis. Insofar as there are data and theory to support it, the preferred framework is formal benefit-cost analysis. If the valuation of nontraded goods is impossible, I favor a regulatory budget approach. If there are insufficient data and theory to allow that framework, either informal benefit-risk or risk-risk analysis should be applied.

Neither the no-risk nor technology-based-standards framework is worthy of further consideration. The former is not acceptable when translated into regulations and the latter is an intellectually bankrupt form of social regulation by engineering intuition.

Making Social Regulation Work

I introduced this book with a Hobbesian choice: Americans can't live with social regulation because of its cost and disruption and can't live without it because of the strong public desire to curb the worst abuses of an industrial economy. Neither of the extreme choices, putting more resources into the regulatory agencies and easing promulgation rules versus eliminating the laws and agencies, is viable. Americans have no choice but to learn to accomplish these social goals with less controversy and greater efficiency.

The difficulties with social regulation stem from many sources. Often the wrong question is presented, or at least the question is so fuzzy that a clear answer is precluded. For example, goals for reducing food contaminants are so fuzzy that virtually any decision could be justified.

Of greater importance is the range of actions permitted the agency and the framework to be used for making decisions. Alternative frameworks require different levels of data and analysis and allow different levels of discretion to the agency. The choice among frameworks depends on social goals, on the state of knowledge within an area, on the availability of data and analysts, and finally on willingness to bear risks and uncertainty. In fact, each decision framework presents a different way of viewing the world. Each emphasizes a particular aspect of data and decisionmaking. No one framework is likely to be best for all decisions, but failure to use the most general one that can be applied to each case results in wasted resources.

The case studies of food additives and of quantitative analyses generally demonstrate that even in the most emotionally laden area analysis helps to clarify the issues. It is precisely in these emotionally laden areas that analysis has the most to offer. Without it, decisions are made on the basis of visceral reactions and emotion. As became clear for sodium nitrite and many aspects of medical care, these reactions and first judgments are often in error, particularly judgments regarding priorities. Resources are squandered because the most effective programs are starved while ineffective or pernicious programs are supported. The prime objective of the analysis is not the bookkeeper's goal of shaving a few dollars from cost but rather to determine which programs are effective so that they can be strengthened and ineffective programs can be eliminated.

Social regulation is in trouble, not because it is too costly, but because it is ineffective in accomplishing social goals. Quantitative analysis, particularly within the regulatory budget framework, offers a chance to make these programs effective. If Congress will require agencies to emphasize data collection and analysis and will itself clarify goals, the major obstacles to intelligent social regulation will have been removed. There will still remain the basic difficulties of conflicting values and scientific uncertainty, but a major step forward will have been taken.

APPENDIX

Implementing the Indirect
Risk-Risk Framework

THE INDIRECT risk-risk framework postulates that society is attempting to minimize the adverse health effects associated with the production and consumption of a commodity, per unit of that commodity. As distinct from the direct risk-risk framework, which is concerned only with risk to consumers, this framework includes risk to workers in producing the commodity.

For example, consider a proposed design change in a plant that is projected to increase construction costs by $200 million and to lead to five fewer accidental deaths among workers over the life of the plant. This framework would note that increased construction means increased risk to workers, since construction is a dangerous occupation. Suppose that construction work involves about one accidental death for every $10 million of activity ($1 \times 10^{-7}$ deaths per dollar of construction). If so, then the proposed design change would be estimated to lead to the deaths of twenty additional workmen in construction and to save five workers after the plant is completed. Obviously this design change is a net loss when considered from an indirect risk-risk perspective.

The example might be extended a bit to a case where the additional construction was designed to remove a food contaminant that is estimated to lead to five deaths among consumers during the lifetime of the plant. If so, the indirect risk-risk framework would again show the design change to be pernicious. Some critics of the approach might argue that allowing the deaths of twenty workers is better than allowing the deaths of five consumers since the former know they are at risk, are compensated for it, and can choose whether to accept the risk.

Implementing this framework is difficult in that there is rarely a pure case where occupational accidents would exceed the proposed benefit. Instead, a regulation leads to the consumption of additional resources spread across a vast number of goods and services. For example, banning diethylstilbestrol as a feed supplement would require more grain to fatten the cattle, more feedlots, and thus more effort from farmers, probably

136

more seed and capital equipment, and more feedlot workers, equipment, and so forth, assuming present practices are continued and beef consumption does not drop. The occupational risk associated with these additional resources might be estimated by taking the accident and disease rates for each occupation (disability days per man-hour) and multiplying them by the estimated increase in man-hours required to grow the additional grain and build and operate the additional feedlots.

This estimation, however, does not account for the steel to produce the additional farm machinery needed to produce the additional grain (assuming beef output is fixed). Thus one would have to estimate the accident and disease disability days associated with producing the capital goods needed to grow and transport the grain and operate the feedlots. Leontief's input-output framework was designed precisely to take account of such second round, or indirect, effects.[1]

The method would be implemented by estimating the direct increases in capital goods and operating costs required to meet the new standard. The input-output framework would be used to translate these direct resource requirements into total resource requirements by estimating the amounts needed to produce the goods used directly (the indirect resource requirements). Productivity levels for each industry would be used to translate the required output of each industry into man-hours required for this production. The final step, going from man-hours to accident and disease disability days, would be taken by applying estimates of the accident and disease disability rates per man-hour to the total number of man-hours used in each industry.

Virtually all the data required for the estimation are currently collected by the government. The Department of Labor collects data both on accident rates and on productivity for each industry.[2] The Department of Commerce maintains a detailed input-output table.[3] Thus putting together the input-output table, productivity figures, and accident rates is straightforward.

Unfortunately occupational disease has been the subject of extensive study only recently. While disease rates might be estimated for a handful

1. Wassily Leontief, *Input-Output Economics*, pp. 13–30.
2. U.S. Department of Labor, Bureau of Labor Statistics, *Occupational Injuries and Illnesses in the United States by Industry, 1976;* and U.S. Department of Labor, Bureau of Labor Statistics, *Productivity Indexes for Selected Industries, 1978 Edition.*
3. U.S. Department of Commerce, *Input-Output Structure of the U.S. Economy: 1967.*

of industries, from coal mining to cotton workers, there are no data for most workers.[4] To implement this framework in the short run, most occupational disease rates would have to be guessed at or set to zero. However, the work of the National Institute of Occupational Safety and Health and the Occupational Safety and Health Administration should enable many more of these disease rates to be estimated over the next several years.

Thus it would be straightforward to estimate accident and some disease disability days immediately and to make a rough guess at other disease rates. The accident and known disease rates would provide a lower estimate of the indirect risks; guesses at occupational disease for other groups would provide better estimates of the indirect risks. This framework could be implemented quickly and relatively cheaply.

4. See the discussion in U.S. Department of Health, Education, and Welfare, *Human Health and the Environment: Some Research Needs*, pp. 55–71. See also Linnea Freeburg, "Epidemiological Studies in Occupational Health: An Annotated Bibliography."

Selected Bibliography

THIS BIBLIOGRAPHY is divided into two parts. Complete citations, listed alphabetically, are given in part A; in part B the same publications are listed under subject headings by author and date only.

A. Alphabetical Listing

Abelson, Philip H. "The Tris Controversy," *Science*, vol. 197 (July 8, 1978).

Ackerman, Bruce A., and others. *The Uncertain Search for Environmental Quality*. New York: Free Press, 1974.

American Meat Institute. "Assessment of Risks from Nitrosopyrrolidine and *Clostridium botulism* in Bacon." Washington, D.C., August 1977.

———. "The Effect of Alpha-Tocopherol on Nitrosamine Formation during Frying of Bacon." Washington, D.C., 1978a.

———. "Summary of Recent Research on Nitrite as It Relates to Botulinal Protection in Cured Meats." Washington, D.C., March 1978(b).

Antonioli, Donald A., Louis Burke, and Emanuel A. Friedman. "Natural History of Diethylstilbestrol-Associated Genital Tract Lesions: Cervical Ectopy and Cervicovaginal Hood," *American Journal of Obstetrics and Gynecology*, vol. 137 (August 1, 1980).

Armitage, P., and R. Doll. "Stochastic Models for Carcinogenesis," in *Proceedings of the Fourth Berkeley Symposium on Mathematics, Statistics and Probability*. Berkeley: University of California Press, 1961.

Armstrong, Bruce, and others. "Cancer Mortality and Saccharin Consumption in Diabetics," *British Journal of Preventive and Social Medicine*, vol. 30 (September 1976).

Arrow, Kenneth J. "Limited Knowledge and Economic Analysis," *American Economic Review*, vol. 64 (March 1974).

———, and F. H. Hahn. *General Competitive Analysis*. San Francisco: Holden-Day, 1971.

———, and Mordecai Kurz. *Public Investment, the Rate of Return, and Optimal Fiscal Policy*. Baltimore: Johns Hopkins University Press for Resources for the Future, 1970.

Arthur Anderson and Company. *Cost of Government Regulation Study for the Business Roundtable*. Executive Summary. Chicago: Arthur Anderson, 1979.

Ashford, Nicholas A. *Crisis in the Workplace: Occupational Injury and Disease*. Cambridge: MIT Press, 1976.

Bailar, John C., and David Byar. "Estrogen Treatment for Cancer of the Prostate: Early Results with 3 Doses of Diethylstilbestrol and Placebo," *Cancer*, vol. 26 (August 1970).

Baram, Michael S. *Alternatives to Regulation for Managing Risks to Health, Safety, and Environment*. Report to the Ford Foundation. Concord, N.H.: Franklin Pierce Law Center, September 1980.

―――. "Regulation of Health, Safety and Environmental Quality and the Use of Cost-Benefit Analysis." Final Report to the Administrative Conference of the United States, March 1979.

Bard, J. C., and Oscar Meyer and Co. "Collaborative USDA, FDA, and AMI Studies on Sodium Nitrate and Sodium Nitrite in Cured Meat Products." Paper presented to the Expert Panel on Nitrites and Nitrosamines, June 27, 1977.

Barnes, Ann B., and others. "Fertility and Outcome of Pregnancy in Women Exposed in Utero to Diethylstilbestrol," *New England Journal of Medicine*, vol. 302 (March 13, 1980).

Barrett, Larry B., and Thomas E. Waddell. *Cost of Air Pollution Damage: A Status Report*. Research Triangle Park, N.C.: U.S. Environmental Protection Agency, 1973.

Bartman, Thomas R. "Benzene." Working Paper. Pittsburgh, Pa.: Carnegie-Mellon University, September 1980.

Baumol, William J. "On the Social Rate of Discount," *American Economic Review*, vol. 58 (June 1968).

Beauchamp, Dan E. "Public Health and Individual Liberty," *Annual Review of Public Health*, vol. 1 (1980).

Belloc, Nedra B. "Relationship of Health Practices and Mortality," *Preventive Medicine*, vol. 2 (January 1973).

―――, and Lester Breslow. "Relationship of Physical Health Status and Health Practices," *Preventive Medicine*, vol. 1 (August 1972).

Berg, Robert L., ed. *Health Status Indexes*. Proceedings of a Conference Conducted by Health Services Research. Chicago: Hospital Research and Educational Trust, 1973.

Bevan, Gwyn, and others. *Health Care: Priorities and Management*. London: Croom Helm, 1980.

Bibbo, Marluce. "Final Progress Report on Contract NIH No. 1-4-2850." Chicago: University of Chicago, August 31, 1977.

―――, and others. "Follow-up Study of Male and Female Offspring of DES-Exposed Mothers," *Journal of the American College of Obstetricians and Gynecologists*, vol. 49 (January 1977).

Blum, Arlene, and Bruce N. Ames. "Flame-Retardant Additives as Possible Cancer Hazards," *Science*, vol. 195 (January 7, 1977).

Booth, Nicholas H. "Written Testimony in the Matter of Diethylstilbestrol: Withdrawal of Approval of New Animal Drug Applications." FDA Docket No. 76N-0002, September 9, 1977.

Breslow, Lester, and James E. Enstrom. "The Persistence of Health Habits and Their Relationship to Mortality," *Preventive Medicine*, vol. 9 (July 1980).

Briggs, Dwight D., and Lester B. Lave. "Risk Assessments of Coke Oven Emissions." Working Paper. Pittsburgh, Pa.: Carnegie-Mellon University, September 1980.

Brook, Robert H., and others. *Conceptualization and Measurement of Health for Adults in the Health Insurance Study.* Vol. 8: *Overview.* Santa Monica, Calif.: RAND Corporation, 1979.

Brookshire, David S., Berry C. Ives, and William D. Schulze. "The Valuation of Aesthetic Preferences." Laramie: University of Wyoming, no date.

Bulow, H. H., and others. "Mamma-Carcinom bei oestrogenbehandeltem Prostata-Carcinom," *Urolege,* vol. A12 (September 1973).

Bunker, John P., Benjamin A. Barnes, and Frederick Mosteller, eds. *Costs, Risks, and Benefits of Surgery.* New York: Oxford University Press, 1977.

Chrisman, C. Larry. "Aneuploidy in Mouse Embryos Induced by Diethylstilbestrol-Diphosphate," *Teratology,* vol. 9 (January 1974).

Chrisman, C. L., and L. L. Hinkel. "Induction of Aneuploidy in Mouse Bone Marrow Cells with Diethylstilbestrol Diphosphate," *Canadian Journal of Genetics and Cytology,* vol. 16 (1974).

Clark, Elizabeth M., and Andrew J. Van Horn. *Risk-Benefit Analysis and Public Policy: A Bibliography.* Rev. ed. Informal Report. Cambridge: Energy and Environmental Policy Center, Harvard University, 1978.

Cohen, Bernard L. "Society Valuation of Life Saving in Radiation Protection and Other Contexts." Working Paper, University of Pittsburgh and Argonne National Laboratory, 1979.

Comar, Cyril. "SO2 Regulations Ignore Costs, Poor Science Base," *Chemical Engineering News,* vol. 57 (April 23, 1979).

Comptroller General of the United States. *Does Nitrite Cause Cancer? Concerns about Validity of FDA-Sponsored Study Delay Answer.* Washington, D.C.: U.S. General Accounting Office, 1980.

Cooper, Barbara S., and Dorothy P. Rice. "The Economic Cost of Illness Revisited," *Social Security Bulletin,* vol. 39 (February 1976).

Council for Agricultural Science and Technology. *Aflatoxin and Other Mycotoxins: An Agricultural Perspective.* Report 80. Ames, Iowa: CAST, 1979.

————. "Comments on the Newberne Report of Dietary Nitrite in the Rat," September 25, 1978.

————. *Hormonally Active Substances in Foods: A Safety Evaluation.* Report 66. Ames, Iowa: CAST, 1977.

————. *Nitrite in Meat Curing: Risks and Benefits.* Report 74. Ames, Iowa: CAST, 1978.

Council on Wage and Price Stability. "Environmental Protection Agency's Proposed Revisions to the National Ambient Air Quality Standard for Photochemical Oxidants." Report of the Regulatory Analysis Review Group, October 1978.

————. "Proposed Standard for Exposure to Cotton Dust." Comments before the Occupational Safety and Health Administration. Docket No. H-052, June 1977.

Crandall, Robert W., and Lester B. Lave, eds. *The Scientific Basis of Health and Safety Regulations*. Washington, D.C.: Brookings Institution, forthcoming.

Crocker, T. D., and others. *Methods of Assessing Air Pollution Control Benefits*. Part I: *Experiments in the Economics of Air Pollution Epidemiology*. Research Triangle Park, N.C.: U.S. Environmental Protection Agency, February 1979.

Crump, K. S. "Estimating Human Risks from Drug Feed Additives." Ruston, La.: Louisiana Technical University, 1978.

Cutler, Bruce S., and others. "Endometrial Carcinoma after Stilbestrol Therapy in Gonadal Dysgenesis," *New England Journal of Medicine*, vol. 287 (September 18, 1972).

Dasgupta, A. K., and D. W. Pierce. *Cost-Benefit Analysis: Theory and Practice*. New York: Barnes and Noble, 1972.

Debreu, Gerard. *Theory of Value: An Axiomatic Analysis of Economic Equilibrium*. New York: Wiley, 1959.

DeLucia, Anthony J., and William C. Adams. "Effects of O_3 Inhalation during Exercise on Pulmonary Function and Blood Biochemistry," *Journal of Applied Physiology: Respiratory, Environmental and Exercise Physiology*, vol. 43 (July 1977).

DeMuth, Christopher C. "Constraining Regulatory Costs." Part 1: "The White House Review Programs," *Regulation*, vol. 4 (January-February 1980[a]).

————. "Constraining Regulatory Costs." Part 2: "The Regulatory Budget," *Regulation*, vol. 4 (March-April 1980[b]).

Denison, Edward F. *Accounting for Slower Economic Growth: The United States in the 1970s*. Washington, D.C.: Brookings Institution, 1979.

Diesler, Paul F., Jr. "Dealing with Industrial Health Risks." Paper presented to the American Association for the Advancement of Science, January 7, 1980.

DiPietro, Aldona. "An Analysis of the OSHA Inspection Program in Manufacturing Industries, 1972–1973." Draft Report to the U.S. Department of Labor, August 1976.

Doniger, David D. *The Law and Policy of Toxic Substances Control: A Case Study of Vinyl Chloride*. Baltimore: Johns Hopkins University Press for Resources for the Future, 1978.

Dreze, Jacques H., ed. *Allocation under Uncertainty: Equilibrium and Optimality*. Proceedings from a Workshop Sponsored by the International Economic Association. New York: Wiley, 1974.

Epple, Dennis, and Lester Lave. "Helium: Investments in the Future," *Bell Journal of Economics*, vol. 11 (Autumn 1980).

Erickson, L. E. "Issues and Experiences in Applying Benefit Cost Analysis to Health and Safety Standards." Final Draft of a Report to the U.S. Nuclear Regulatory Commission. Richland, Wash.: Battelle Pacific Northwest Laboratories, September 1977.

Fassett, D. W. "Nitrates and Nitrites," in National Academy of Sciences, *Toxicants Occurring Naturally in Foods*. 2d ed. Washington, D.C.: NAS, 1973.

Fine, D. D., and others. "N-Nitroso Compounds in Air and Water." Paper presented at the International Agency for Research on Cancer meeting, October 1975.

Fischoff, Baruch, and others. "Approaches to Acceptable Risk." Preliminary Draft of a Report to the Nuclear Regulatory Commission, 1980.

Fitzsimons, M. P. "Gynaecomastia in Stilbestrol Workers," *British Journal of Independent Medicine*, vol. 1 (October 1944).

Freeburg, Linnea. "Epidemiological Studies in Occupational Health: An Annotated Bibliography." Pittsburgh, Pa.: Carnegie-Mellon University, 1980.

Freeman, A. Myrick, III. "The Benefits of Air and Water Pollution Control: A Review and Synthesis of Recent Estimates." Report prepared for the Council on Environmental Quality, December 1979.

———. *The Benefits of Environmental Improvement: Theory and Practice.* Baltimore: Johns Hopkins University Press for Resources for the Future, 1979.

Friedman, Milton. *Capitalism and Freedom.* Chicago: University of Chicago Press, 1962.

Fuchs, Victor R. "Economics, Health, and Post Industrial Society," *Milbank Memorial Fund Quarterly,* vol. 57 (Spring 1979).

———. "Some Economic Aspects of Mortality in Developed Countries," in Mark Perlman, ed., *The Economics of Health and Medical Care.* New York: Wiley, 1974.

Galbraith, John Kenneth. *Economics and the Public Purpose.* Boston: Houghton Mifflin, 1973.

———. *The New Industrial State,* 3d ed. Boston: Houghton Mifflin, 1979.

Gass, George H. "A Discussion of Assay Sensitivity Methodology and Carcinogenic Potential," *Food-Drug-Cosmetic Law Journal,* vol. 30 (February 1975).

———, Don Coats, and Nora Graham. "Carcinogenic Dose-Response Curve to Oral Diethylstilbestrol," *Journal of the National Cancer Institute,* vol. 33 (December 1964).

Gaylor, David W., and Raymond E. Shapiro. "Extrapolation and Risk Estimation for Carcinogenesis," in Myron A. Mehlman, Raymond E. Shapiro, and Herbert Blumenthal, eds. *Advances in Modern Toxicology.* Vol. 1: *New Concepts in Safety Evaluation.* New York: Wiley, 1979.

Gianessi, Leonard P., and Henry M. Peskin. "The Distribution of the Costs of Federal Water Pollution Control Policy," *Land Economics,* vol. 56 (February 1980).

Gill, W. B., Gebhard Schumacher, and Marluce Bibbo. "Structural and Functional Abnormalities in Sex Organs of Male Offspring of Mothers Treated with Diethylstilbestrol (DES)," *Journal of Reproductive Medicine,* vol. 16 (April 1976).

Goldstein, Bernard David. "Experimental and Clinical Problems of Effects of Photochemical Pollutants." Rutgers Medical School, June 1980.

Goldzieher, M. A., and J. W. Goldzieher. "Toxic Effects of Percutaneously

Absorbed Estrogens," *Journal of the American Medical Association,* vol. 40 (August 6, 1949).

Gori, Gio Batta. "The Regulation of Carcinogenic Hazards," *Science,* vol. 208 (April 18, 1980).

Graham, John D., and James W. Vaupel. "The Value of Life: What Difference Does It Make?" *International Journal of Risk Analysis,* vol. 1 (forthcoming).

Green, Laura. "A Risk/Risk Analysis for Nitrite." Working Paper. Cambridge: Massachusetts Institute of Technology, Department of Nutritional Food Science, 1978.

Harberger, A. C., and others, eds. *Benefit-Cost Analysis, 1971.* Chicago: Aldine, 1972.

Harris, Robert H. "The Tris Ban," *Science,* vol. 197 (September 16, 1977).

Harvey, Donald C., and others. "Survey of Food Products for Volatile N-Nitrosamines," *Journal of the AOAC,* vol. 59 (1976).

Haveman, R. H., and others, eds. *Benefit-Cost and Policy Analysis, 1973.* Chicago: Aldine, 1974.

Headley, J. C. "Economic Aspects of Drug and Chemical Feed Additives." Columbia, Mo.: University of Missouri, 1978.

Heilbroner, Robert L. *The Limits of American Capitalism.* New York: Harper and Row, 1965.

Heinonen, Olli P. "Diethylstilbestrol in Pregnancy: Frequency of Exposure and Usage Patterns," *Cancer,* vol. 32 (March 1973).

————, and others. "Cardiovascular Birth Defects and Antenatal Exposure to Female Sex Hormones," *New England Journal of Medicine,* vol. 298 (January 13, 1977).

Herbst, A. L. "Summary of the Changes in the Human Female Genital Tract as a Consequence of Maternal Diethylstilbestrol Therapy," *Journal of Toxicology and Environmental Health,* Supplement 1 (1976).

————, and others. "Age-Incidence and Risk of Diethylstilbestrol-Related Clear Cell Adenocarcinoma of the Vagina and Cervix," *American Journal of Obstetrics and Gynecology,* vol. 128 (May 1977).

————, and others. "Clear-Cell Adenocarcinoma of the Vagina and Cervix in Girls: Analysis of 1970 Registry Cases," *Journal of Obstetric Gynecology,* vol. 119 (July 1974).

Herbst, Arthur L., Robert E. Scully, and Stanley J. Robboy. "The Significance of Adenosis and Clear Cell Adenocarcinoma of the Genital Tract in Young Females," *Journal of Reproductive Medicine,* vol. 15 (July 1975).

Hertz, Roy. "Accidental Ingestion of Estrogens by Children," *Pediatrics,* vol. 21 (February 1958).

————. "Written Direct Testimony in the Matter of Diethylstilbestrol: Withdrawal of Approval of New Animal Drug Applications." FDA Docket No. 76N-0002, 1977.

Higgins, Ian T. T. "Commentary: Smoking and Cancer," *American Journal of Public Health,* vol. 66 (February 1976).

Hitch, Charles J., and Roland N. McKean. *The Economics of Defense in the Nuclear Age.* Cambridge: Harvard University Press, 1960.

Hoel, D. G. "Human Risk Assessment on Laboratory Animal Studies," *Second Joint U.S./U.S.S.R. Symposium on the Comprehensive Analysis of the Environment.* Washington, D.C.: Government Printing Office, 1975.

————. "Statistical Extrapolation Methods for Estimating Risks from Animal Data," *Annals of the New York Academy of Sciences,* vol. 271 (1976).

————. "Statistical Models for Estimating Carcinogenic Risks from Animal Data," *Proceedings of the Fifth Annual Conference on Environmental Toxicology.* Washington, D.C.: Government Printing Office, 1974.

Holland, W. W., and others. "Health Effects of Particulate Pollution: Reappraising the Evidence," *American Journal of Epidemiology,* vol. 110 (June 1979).

Holtzman, Neil A., Allen G. Meek, and E. David Mellits. "Neonatal Screening for Phenylketonuria." Part 1: "Effectiveness," *Journal of the American Medical Association,* vol. 229 (August 5, 1974).

Hoover, Robert. "Saccharin: Bitter Aftertaste," *New England Journal of Medicine,* vol. 302 (March 6, 1980).

————, and others. "Progress Report to the Food and Drug Administration from the National Cancer Institute Concerning the National Bladder Cancer Study." Bethesda, Md.: National Cancer Institute, 1979.

Huelke, Donald F., and others. *Effectiveness of Current and Future Restraint Systems in Fatal and Serious Injury Automobile Crashes.* Society of Automotive Engineers. Technical Report 790323. Detroit: SAE, 1979.

Huggins, C., and C. V. Hodges. "Studies in Prostatic Cancer." Part I: "The Effects of Castration, of Estrogen and of Androgen Injection on Serum Phosphates in Metastatic Carcinoma of the Prostate," *Cancer Research,* vol. 1 (December 1941).

Hutt, Peter Barton. "Food Regulation," *Food-Drug-Cosmetic Law Journal,* vol. 33 (October 1978).

Interagency Regulatory Liaison Group. "Scientific Bases for Identifying Potential Carcinogens and Estimating Their Risks." Report of the IRLG Work Group on Risk Assessment, 1979.

Ivey, F. J., and others. "Effect of Potassium Sorbate on Toxinogenesis of *Clostridium botulinum* in Bacon," in American Meat Institute, *Response for Bacon: Nitrates and Nitrites in Meat Products, Requests for Data, Federal Register, October 18, 1977.* Tab 26, 1978.

Jensen, Elwood V. "Written Direct Testimony in the Matter of Diethylstilbestrol: Withdrawal of Approval of New Animal Drug Applications." FDA Docket No. 76N-0002, August 16, 1977.

Jones, H. B., and A. Grendon. "Environmental Factors in the Origin of Cancer and Estimation of the Possible Hazard to Man," *Food and Cosmetic Toxicology,* vol. 13 (March 1975).

Jones, H. W., and W. W. Scot. *Hermaphroditism, Genital Anomalies and Related Endocrine Disorders.* 2d ed. Baltimore: Williams and Wilkins, 1971.

Jukes, Thomas H. "Diethylstilbestrol in Beef Production: What is the Risk?" *Preventive Medicine,* vol. 5 (June 1976).

————. "Testimony in the Matter of Diethylstilbestrol: Withdrawal of New Animal Drug Applications." FDA Docket No. 76N-0002, September 1977.

Keeler, Theodore E. "Domestic Trunk Airline Deregulation: An Economic Evaluation," in U.S. Congress. Senate. Committee on Governmental Affairs. *Study on Federal Regulation*. Vol. 6: *Framework for Regulation*. Appendix. 96 Cong. 1 sess. Washington, D.C.: Government Printing Office, 1978.

Kendall, J., and D. Kriebe. "Carcinogen File: The Ames Test," *Environment*, vol. 21 (January 1978).

Kennedy, B. J. "Hormone Therapy in Inoperable Breast Cancer," *Cancer*, vol. 24 (December 1969).

Kessler, Irving I. "Cancer Mortality Among Diabetics," *Journal of the National Cancer Institute*, vol. 44 (March 1970).

Kliman, Bernard. "Testimony in the Matter of Diethylstilbestrol: Withdrawal of Approval of New Animal Drug Applications." FDA Docket No. 76N-0002, September 1977.

Kneese, Allen V., and Blair T. Bower. *Environmental Quality and Residuals Management*. Baltimore: Johns Hopkins University Press for Resources for the Future, 1979.

Kraybill, H. F. "Conceptual Approaches to the Assessment of Nonoccupational Environmental Cancer," in H. F. Kraybill and Myron A. Mehlman, eds. *Advances in Modern Toxicology*. Vol. 3: *Environmental Cancer*. New York: Wiley, 1977.

Kuchera, Lucile K. "Postcoital Contraception with Diethylstilbestrol—Updated," *Contraception*, vol. 10 (May 1974).

Land, Charles E. "Informal Public Hearing Re: Proposed Standard for Coke Oven Emissions." U.S. Department of Labor, Occupational Safety and Health Administration, May 4, 1976.

Lassiter, Donald V. "Occupational Carcinogenesis," in H. F. Kraybill and Myron A. Mehlman, eds. *Advances in Modern Toxicology*. Vol. 3: *Environmental Cancer*. New York: Wiley, 1977.

Lave, Lester B. "Air Pollution Damage: Some Difficulties in Estimating the Value of Abatement," in Allen V. Kneese and Blair T. Bower, eds., *Environmental Quality Analysis: Theory and Method in the Social Sciences*. Baltimore: Johns Hopkins University Press for Resources for the Future, 1972.

————. "Conflicting Objectives in Regulating the Automobile: The Interdependence of Safety, Emissions and Fuel Economy," *Science* (forthcoming).

————. "Health, Safety, and Environmental Regulations," in Joseph A. Pechman, ed., *Setting National Priorities: Agenda for the 1980s*. Washington, D.C.: Brookings Institution, 1980.

————, and Judith R. Lave. "Empirical Studies of Hospital Cost Functions: A Review," in George Chacko, ed. *Health Handbook*. New York, Amsterdam, London: North-Holland, 1979.

————, and Eugene P. Seskin. *Air Pollution and Human Health*. Baltimore: Johns Hopkins University Press for Resources for the Future, 1977.

————, and ————. "Epidemiology, Causality, and Public Policy," *American Scientist*, vol. 67 (March-April 1979).

————, and Lester Silverman. "Economic Costs of Energy-Related Environmental Pollution," *Annual Review of Energy,* vol. 1 (1976).

————, and others. "Economic Impact of Preventive Medicine," in *Preventive Medicine USA.* Task Force Reports sponsored by the John E. Fogarty International Center for Advanced Study in the Health Sciences, National Institutes of Health, and the American College of Preventive Medicine. New York: Prodist, 1976.

————, and Warren E. Weber. "A Benefit-Cost Analysis of Auto Safety Features," *Applied Economics,* vol. 2 (October 1970).

Lenard, Thomas M. "Lawn Mower Safety," in James C. Miller III and Bruce Yandle, eds. *Benefit-Cost Analyses of Social Regulation: Case Studies from the Council on Wage and Price Stability.* Washington, D.C.: American Enterprise Institute for Public Policy Research, 1979.

Leontief, Wassily. *Input-Output Economics.* New York: Oxford University Press, 1966.

Levy, Bert. "Testimony in the Matter of Diethylstilbestrol: Withdrawal of Approval of New Animal Drug Applications." FDA Docket No. 76-0002, September 1977.

Lijinsky, William. "Current Concepts in The Toxicology of Nitrates, Nitrites, and Nitrosamines," in Myron A. Mehlman, Raymond E. Shapiro, and Herbert Blumenthal, eds. *Advances in Modern Toxicology.* Vol. 1: *New Concepts in Safety Evaluation.* New York: Wiley, 1979.

————. "Health Problems Associated with Nitrites and Nitrosamines," in U.S. Congress. Senate. Committee on Agriculture, Nutrition, and Forestry. Subcommittee on Agricultural Research and General Legislation. *Food Safety and Quality: Nitrites.* Hearings. 95 Cong. 2 sess. Washington, D.C.: Government Printing Office, 1978.

————. "Standard Setting for Nitrites and Nitrosamines," in Howard H. Hiatt, James D. Watson, and Jay A. Winston, eds. *Origins of Human Cancer.* 4 vols. Cold Spring Harbor, New York: Cold Spring Harbor Laboratory, 1977.

Linnerooth, Joanne. "The Value of Human Life: A Review of the Models," *Economic Inquiry,* vol. 17 (January 1979).

Lipfert, F. W. "Differential Mortality and the Environment: The Challenge of Multicollinearity in Cross-Sectional Studies," *Energy Systems and Policy,* vol. 3, no. 3 (1980).

Lloyd, William J. "Long-Term Mortality Study of Steelworkers." Part 4: "Mortality by Work Area," *Journal of Occupational Medicine,* vol. 12 (May 1970).

————. "Long-Term Mortality Study of Steelworkers." Part 5: "Respiratory Cancer in Coke Plant Workers," *Journal of Occupational Medicine,* vol. 13 (February 1971).

————, and Antonio Ciocco. "Long-Term Mortality Study of Steelworkers." Part 1: "Methodology," *Journal of Occupational Medicine,* vol. 11 (June 1969).

Lowrance, William W. *Of Acceptable Risk: Science and the Determination of Safety.* Los Altos, Calif.: William Kaufmann, 1976.

MacAvoy, Paul W., and John W. Snow, eds. *Railroad Revitalization and Regulatory Reform.* Washington, D.C.: American Enterprise Institute for Public Policy Research, 1977.

McCarrol, A. M., and others. "Endometrial Carcinoma after Cyclical Oestrogen-Progestogen Therapy for Turner's Syndrome," *British Journal of Obstetrics and Gynecology,* vol. 82 (July 1975).

McLachlan, John A. "Written Testimony in the Matter of Diethylstilbestrol." FDA Docket No. 76-0002, March 24, 1977.

———, and Robert L. Dixon. "Transplacental Toxicity of Diethylstilbestrol: A Special Problem in Safety Evaluation," in Myron A. Mehlman, Raymond E. Shapiro, and Herbert Blumenthal, eds., *Advances in Modern Toxicology.* Vol. 1: *Concepts in Safety Evaluation.* New York: Wiley, 1978.

Magee, P. N., R. Montesano, and R. Preussmann. "N-Nitroso Compounds and Related Carcinogens," in Charles E. Searle, ed. *Chemical Carcinogens.* American Chemical Society Monograph 173. Washington, D.C.: ACS, 1976.

Mancuso, Thomas K., Alice Stewart, and George Kneale. "Radiation Exposures of Hanford Workers Dying from Cancer and Other Causes," *Health Physics,* vol. 33 (November 1977).

Mantel, N., and W. R. Bryan. "Safety Testing of Carcinogenic Agents," *Journal of the National Cancer Institute,* vol. 27 (August 1960).

———, and others. "An Improved Mantel-Bryan Procedure for 'Safety' Testing of Carcinogens," *Cancer Research,* vol. 35 (1975).

Marnicio, Ronald J. "An Examination of the Application of Quantitative Risk Analysis to Ionizing Radiation as Done by the Environmental Protection Agency for 40 CFR Part 190." Working Paper. Pittsburgh, Pa.: Carnegie-Mellon University, September 1980.

Marraro, Christopher. "The Revision of the Photochemical Oxidant (Ozone) Standard." Working Paper. Pittsburgh, Pa.: Carnegie-Mellon University, September 1980.

Martin, A. I. E. "Mortality and Morbidity Statistics and Air Pollution," *Proceedings of the Royal Society of Medicine,* vol. 21 (1964).

Mazumdar, Sati, and Carol K. Redmond. "Evaluating Dose-Response Relationships Using Epidemiological Data on Occupational Subgroups," in Norman E. Breslow and Anne S. Whittemore, eds. *Energy and Health: Proceedings of a Siam Institute for Mathematics and Society Conference.* Philadelphia: Society for Industrial and Applied Mathematics, 1979.

Mendeloff, John. "An Evaluation of the OSHA Program's Effect on Workplace Injury Rates: Evidence from California through 1974." Report for the U.S. Department of Labor, July 1976.

Merrill, Richard A. "Federal Regulation of Cancer Causing Chemicals." Draft Report to the Administrative Conference of the United States, 1980.

———. "Regulating Carcinogens in Food: A Legislator's Guide to the Food

Safety Provisions of the Federal Food, Drug, and Cosmetic Act," *Michigan Law Review,* vol. 77 (December 1978).

Miller, James C., III. "Exposure to Coke Oven Emissions Proposed Standard." Statement on behalf of the Council of Wage and Price Stability, before the Occupational Safety and Health Administration. Docket No. H-017A, May 1976.

Mirvish, S. S. "Formation of N-Nitroso Compounds: Chemistry, Kinetics, and *in Vivo* Occurrence," *Toxicology and Applied Pharmacology,* vol. 31 (May 31, 1975).

Mishan, E. J. *Cost-Benefit Analysis: New and Expanded Edition.* New York: Praeger, 1976.

Mitchell, Robert Cameron. "Silent Spring/Solid Majorities," *Public Opinion,* vol. 2 (August-September 1979).

Morgan, M. Granger, Max Henrion, and Samuel C. Morris. "Expert Judgements for Policy Analysis." Report of an Invitational Workshop Held at Brookhaven National Laboratory, July 8–11, 1979. Pittsburgh, Pa.: Carnegie-Mellon University, 1979.

—————, and others. "Sulfur Control in Coal Fired Power Plants: A Probabilistic Approach to Policy Analysis," *Journal of the Air Pollution Control Association,* vol. 28 (October 1978).

Morrell, M. T., and S. C. Truelove. "Congestive Cardiac Failure Induced by Oestrogen Therapy," *Postgraduate Medical Journal,* vol. 38 (March 1962).

Morrison, Alan S., and Julie E. Buring. "Artificial Sweeteners and Cancer of the Lower Urinary Tract," *New England Journal of Medicine,* vol. 302 (March 6, 1980).

National Academy of Sciences. Advisory Committee on the Biological Effects of Ionizing Radiations. *The Effects on Populations of Exposures to Low Levels of Ionizing Radiation.* Washington, D.C.: NAS, 1979a.

—————. Commission on Natural Resources. *Nitrites: An Environmental Assessment.* Washington, D.C.: NAS, 1978a.

—————. Committee on the Biological Effects of Ionizing Radiations. *The Effects on Populations of Exposure to Low Levels of Ionizing Radiation.* Washington, D.C.: NAS, 1980.

—————. Committee on Environmental Decision Making. *Analytical Studies for the U.S. Environmental Protection Agency.* Vol. 2: *Decision Making in the Environmental Protection Agency.* Washington, D.C.: NAS, 1977.

—————. Committee on Impacts of Stratospheric Change. *Protection against Depletion of Stratospheric Ozone by Chlorofluorocarbons.* Washington, D.C.: NAS, 1979b.

—————. Committee on Mineral Resources and the Environment. *Mineral Resources and the Environment, Supplementary Report, Coal Worker Pneumoconiosis: Medical Considerations, Some Social Implications.* Washington, D.C.: NAS, 1976.

—————. Committee on Principles of Decision Making for Chemicals in the Environment. *Decision Making for Regulating Chemicals in the Environment.* Washington, D.C.: NAS, 1975.

————. Committee for a Study on Saccharin and Food Safety Policy. *Food Safety Policy: Scientific and Societal Considerations.* Washington, D.C.: NAS, 1979c.

————. ————. *Saccharin: Technical Assessment of Risks and Benefits.* Washington, D.C.: NAS, 1978b.

————. Committee on Sulfur Oxides. *Sulfur Oxides.* Washington, D.C.: NAS, 1978c.

————. *Energy in Transition 1985–2010: Final Report of the Committee on Nuclear and Alternative Energy Systems.* San Francisco: Freeman, 1979d.

————. National Academy of Engineering. *Product Safety.* Washington, D.C.: Government Printing Office, 1972.

————. National Research Council. *Energy Modeling for an Uncertain Future: The Report of the Model Resource Group Synthesis Panel of the Committee on Nuclear and Alternative Energy Systems.* Supporting Paper 2. Study of Nuclear and Alternative Energy Systems. Washington, D.C.: NAS, 1978d.

National Safety Council. *Accident Facts, 1980 Edition.* Chicago: NSC, 1980.

Newberne, Paul M. "Dietary Nitrite in the Rat." Cambridge: Massachusetts Institute of Technology, May 1978(e).

————. "Nitrite Promotes Lymphoma Incidence in Rats," *Science,* vol. 204 (June 8, 1979[e]).

Niskanen, W. A., and others, eds. *Benefit-Cost Policy Analysis, 1972.* Chicago: Aldine, 1973.

Noll, Roger G. *Reforming Regulation: An Evaluation of the Ash Council Proposals.* Washington, D.C.: Brookings Institution, 1971.

Noller, K. L., and C. R. Fish. "Diethylstilbestrol Usage: Its Interesting Past, Important Present, and Questionable Future," *Medical Clinics of North America,* vol. 58 (July 1974).

Nordhaus, William, and Robert Litan. "A Regulatory Budget for the United States." Washington, D.C.: Brookings Institution, 1981.

Ogilvie, M. L., and others. "Effects of Stilbestrol in Altering Carcass Composition and Feed Lot Performance of Beef Steers," *Journal of Animal Science,* vol. 19 (1960).

Omenn, Gilbert S., and Robert D. Friedman. "Individual Differences in Susceptibility and Regulation of Environmental Hazards," Staff Paper. Office of Science and Technology Policy, 1980.

Pagani, C. "Sindromi iperstriniche de origine esogena osservazioni in lavoratori addetti alla sintesi di sostanze estrogene e quadri sperimentali sull'animale," *Annali di Ostetricia e Ginecologia,* vol. 75 (1953).

Patrick, D. L., J. W. Bush, and M. M. Chen. "Toward an Operational Definition of Health," *Journal of Health and Social Behavior,* vol. 14 (January 1973).

Peers, F. G., and C. A. Linsell. "Dietary Aflatoxins and Liver Cancer: A Population Based Study in Kenya," *British Journal of Cancer,* vol. 27 (June 1973).

Peskin, Henry M., and Eugene P. Seskin, eds. *Cost Benefit Analysis and Water Pollution Policy.* Washington, D.C.: Urban Institute, 1975.

Preussmann, R., and others. "Dose-Response Study with N-Nitrosopyrrolidine and Some Comments on Risk Evaluation of the N-Nitroso Compounds," *Proceedings of the Second International Symposium on Nitrite Meat Production.* Zeist, 1976.

Prunella, Warren J. "A Qualitative Assessment of Cost-Benefit Analysis and Its Application in the Area of Product Safety." Draft Report to the Consumer Product Safety Commission, no date.

Raabe, Otto G., Steven A. Book, and Norris J. Parks. "Bone Cancer from Radium: Canine Dose Response Explains Data for Mice and Humans," *Science,* vol. 208 (April 4, 1980).

Radomski, J. L. "Evaluating the Role of Environmental Chemicals in Human Cancer," in Myron A. Mehlman, Raymond E. Shapiro, and Herbert Blumenthal, eds., *Advances in Modern Toxicology.* Vol. 1: *New Concepts in Safety Evaluation.* New York: Wiley, 1979.

Rai, Kamta, and John Van Ryzin. "Risk Assessment of Toxic Environmental Substances Using a Generalized Multi-Hit Dose Response Model," in Norman E. Breslow and Alice S. Whittemore, eds. *Energy and Health.* Philadelphia: Society for Industry and Applied Mathematics, 1979.

Raiffa, Howard. *Decision Analysis: Introductory Lectures on Choice under Uncertainty.* Reading, Mass.: Addison-Wesley, 1968.

————, William B. Schwartz, and Milton C. Weinstein. "Evaluating Health Effects of Societal Decisions and Programs," in National Academy of Sciences, Committee on Environmental Decision Making, *Analytical Studies for the U.S. Environmental Protection Agency.* Vol. 2b: *Decision Making in the Environmental Protection Agency: Selected Working Papers.* Washington, D.C.: NAS, 1977.

Redmond, Carol K., and others. "Long-Term Mortality Study of Steelworkers." Part 3: "Follow-Up," *Journal of Occupational Medicine,* vol. 11 (October 1969).

————, and ————. "Long-Term Mortality Study of Steelworkers." Part 6: "Mortality from Malignant Neoplasms among Coke Oven Workers," *Journal of Occupational Medicine,* vol. 14 (August 1972).

Reid, D. D., and Carol L. Buck. "Cancer in Coking Plant Workers," *British Journal of Industrial Medicine,* vol. 13 (October 1956).

Rice, Dorothy P., Jacob I. Feldman, and Kerr L. White. "The Current Burden of Illness in the United States." An Occasional Paper of the Institute of Medicine. Washington, D.C.: National Academy of Sciences, 1976.

Rice, D. P., and T. A. Hodgson. "Social and Economic Implications of Cancer in the United States," *World Health Statistics,* vol. 33 (1980). (National Center for Health Statistics Reprint.)

Robinson, Harry. "Long-Term Mortality Study of Steelworkers." Part 2: "Mortality by Income in Whites and Non-Whites," *Journal of Occupational Medicine,* vol. 11 (August 1969).

Rowe, Robert D., Ralph C. d'Arge, and David S. Brookshire. "An Experiment on the Economic Value of Visibility," *Journal of Environmental Economics and Management* (March 1980).

Rowe, William D. *An Anatomy of Risk.* New York: Wiley, 1977.

Ruff, Larry E. "Federal Environmental Regulation," *Study on Federal Regulation.* Vol. 6: *Framework for Regulation.* Appendix. Senate. Committee on Governmental Affairs. 96 Cong. 1 sess. Washington, D.C.: Government Printing Office, 1978.

Rumsey, T. S., and others. "Depletion Patterns of Radioactivity and Tissue Residues in Beef Cattle after Withdrawal of Oral ^{14}C-Diethylstilbestrol," *Journal of Animal Sciences,* vol. 40 (March 1975).

Sackett, David L. "Screening for Early Detection of Disease to What Purpose?" *Bulletin of the New York Academy of Medicine,* vol. 51 (January 1975).

Schelling, T. C. "The Life You Save May Be Your Own," in Samuel B. Chase, ed. *Problems in Public Expenditure Analysis.* Washington, D.C.: Brookings Institution, 1968.

Schoettlin, Charles E., and Emanuel Landau. "Air Pollution and Asthmatic Attacks in the Los Angeles Area," *Public Health Reports,* vol. 76 (June 1961).

Schwing, Richard C. "Expenditures to Reduce Mortality Risk and Increase Longevity." Working Paper, GMR-2353-A. Warren, Mich.: General Motors Research Laboratories, February 22, 1978.

———, and Walter A. Albers, Jr., eds. *Societal Risk Assessment: How Safe is Safe Enough.* New York: Plenum Press, 1980.

Selikoff, Irving J., E. Cuyler Hammond, and Jacob Churq. "Asbestos Exposure, Smoking, and Neoplasia," *Journal of the American Medical Association,* vol. 204 (April 8, 1968).

Shank, R. C., and Paul M. Newberne. "Dose-Response Study of Carcinogenicity of Dietary Sodium Nitrite Morpholine in Rats and Hamsters," *Food and Cosmetic Toxicology,* vol. 14 (January 1976).

Shank, Ronald C. "Epidemiology of Aflatoxin Carcinogenesis," in H. F. Kraybill and Myron A. Mehlman, eds. *Advances in Modern Toxicology.* Vol. 3: *Environmental Cancer.* New York: Wiley, 1977.

Sheeler, Philip. "Testimony in the Matter of Diethylstilbestrol: Withdrawal of Approval of New Animal Drug Applications." FDA Docket No. 76-0002, March 25, 1977.

Shellenberger, Thomas E. "Animal Experiments with Hormones Relevant to Experience in Humans," in Myron A. Mehlman, Raymond E. Shapiro, and Herbert Blumenthal, eds. *Advances in Modern Toxicology.* Vol. 1: *New Concepts in Safety Evaluation.* New York: Wiley, 1979.

Simon, Herbert A. "Spurious Correlation: A Causal Interpretation," *American Statistical Association Journal,* vol. 49 (September 1954).

Smith, R. Jeffrey. "Nitrites: FDA Beats a Surprising Retreat," *Science,* vol. 209 (September 5, 1980).

Smith, Robert S. "Compensating Wage Differentials and Public Policy: A Review." Working Paper. New York State School of Industrial and Labor Relations, Cornell University, November 1978.

Smith, Robert Stewart. *The Occupational Safety and Health Act: Its Goals and Achievements*. Washington, D.C.: American Enterprise Institute for Public Policy Research, 1976.

Starfield, Barbara, and Neil A. Holtzman. "A Comparison of Effectiveness of Screening for Phenylketonuria in the United States, United Kingdom, and Ireland," *New England Journal of Medicine*, vol. 293 (July 17, 1975).

Starr, Chauncey. "Benefit-Cost Studies in Sociotechnical Systems," *Perspectives on Benefit Cost Decision Making*. Washington, D.C.: National Academy of Engineering, 1971.

————. "Social Benefit versus Technological Risk," *Science*, vol. 165 (September 19, 1969).

Sterling, Theodor D. "Additional Comments on the Critical Assessment of the Evidence Bearing on Smoking as the Cause of Lung Cancer," *American Journal of Public Health*, vol. 6 (February 1966).

————. "A Critical Reassessment of the Evidence Bearing on Smoking as the Cause of Lung Cancer," *American Journal of Public Health*, vol. 65 (September 1975).

Stigler, George J. *The Citizen and the State: Essays on Regulation*. Chicago: University of Chicago Press, 1975.

————. "The Cost of Subsistence," *Journal of Farm Economics*, vol. 27 (May 1945).

Stocks, P. "Recent Epidemiological Studies of Lung Cancer Mortality, Cigarette Smoking, and Air Pollution, with Discussion of a New Hypothesis of Causation," *British Journal of Cancer*, vol. 20 (1967).

Stowell, Carol, and Joseph Bryant. *Safety Belt Usage: Survey of Cars in the Traffic Population*. Washington, D.C.: National Highway Traffic Safety Administration, 1978.

Tannenbaum, S. R., and others. "Nitrite and Nitrate Are Formed by Endogenous Synthesis in the Human Intestine," *Science*, vol. 200 (June 30, 1978[a]).

Tannenbaum, Steven R. "Relative Risk Assessment," in Myron A. Mehlman, Raymond F. Shapiro, and Herbert Blumenthal, eds. *Advances in Modern Toxicology*. Vol. 1: *New Concepts in Safety Evaluation*. New York: Wiley, 1979.

————, and others. "Nitrosamine Formation in Human Saliva," *Journal of the National Cancer Institute*, vol. 60 (February 1978[b]).

Terrill, James G. "Cost-Benefit Estimates for the Major Sources of Radiation," *American Journal of Public Health*, vol. 62 (July 1972).

Thaler, Richard, and Sherwin Rosen. "The Value of Saving a Life: Evidence from the Labor Market," in Nestor E. Terleckyj, ed., *Household Production and Consumption*. New York: National Bureau of Economic Research, 1976.

Thibodeau, L. A., R. B. Reed, and Y. M. M. Bishop. "Air Pollution and Human Health: A Review and Reanalysis," *Environmental Health Perspectives,* vol. 34 (February 1980).

U.S. Congress. House. Committee on Interstate and Foreign Commerce. Subcommittee on Oversight and Investigations. *Federal Regulation and Regulatory Reform.* Report. 94 Cong. 2 sess. Washington, D.C.: Government Printing Office, 1976.

———. Senate. Committee on Agriculture, Nutrition, and Forestry. Subcommittee on Agricultural Research and General Legislation. *Food Safety and Quality: Nitrites.* Hearings. 95 Cong. 2 sess. Washington, D.C.: Government Printing Office, 1978.

U.S. Department of Commerce. *Regulatory Reform Seminar: Proceedings and Background Paper.* Washington, D.C.: Government Printing Office, 1979.

———. Bureau of Economic Analysis. *Input-Output Structure of the U.S. Economy: 1967.* Washington, D.C.: Government Printing Office, 1974.

U.S. Department of Energy. *Carbon Dioxide Effects Research and Assessment Program: Workshop on Environmental and Societal Consequences of a Possible Co-Induced Climate Change.* Washington, D.C.: DOE, 1980.

U.S. Department of Health, Education, and Welfare. Center for Disease Control. *Botulism in the United States 1899–1977: Handbook for Epidemiologists, Clinicians and Laboratory Workers.* Atlanta, Ga.: CDC, 1979.

———. National Institute of Environmental Health Sciences. *Human Health and the Environment: Some Research Needs.* Washington, D.C.: Government Printing Office, 1977.

U.S. Department of Labor. Bureau of Labor Statistics. *Occupational Injuries and Illnesses in the United States by Industry, 1976.* Bulletin 2019. Washington, D.C.: Government Printing Office, 1979.

———. ———. *Productivity Indexes for Selected Industries, 1978 Edition.* Bulletin 2002. Washington, D.C.: Government Printing Office, 1978.

U.S. Department of Transportation. Federal Aviation Administration. *Establishment Criteria for Category I Instrument Landing System (ILS).* Washington, D.C.: FAA, December 1975.

———. ———. *Installation Criteria for the Approach Lighting System Improvement Plan (ALSIP).* Washington, D.C.: FAA, 1978.

———. National Highway Traffic Safety Administration. "Preliminary Evaluation of the Proposed Extension of Standards No. 201, 203, and 204 in Light Trucks, Buses, and Multipurpose Passenger Vehicles." Report, November 6, 1978.

U.S. Environmental Protection Agency. *Assessment of Health Effects of Benzene Germane to Low Level Exposure.* Research Triangle Park, N.C.: EPA, 1978.

———. *Assessment of Human Exposures to Atmospheric Benzene.* Research Triangle Park, N.C.: EPA, 1978.

———. *The Cost of Clean Air and Water.* Report to Congress. Research Triangle Park, N.C.: EPA, August 1979(a).

———. *Protecting Visibility: An EPA Report to Congress.* Research Triangle Park, N.C.: EPA, October 1979(b).

U.S. Food and Drug Administration. "Assessment of Estimated Risk Resulting from Aflatoxins in Consumer Peanut Products and Other Food Commodities." Washington, D.C.: FDA, January 19, 1978.

———. "Initial Decision: Proposal to Withdraw Applications for Diethylstilbestrol." Docket No. 76N-0002, September 1977.

———. *Re-evaluation of the Pathology Findings of Studies on Nitrite and Cancer: Histologic Lessons in Sprague Dawley Rats, Final Report.* Washington, D.C.: U.S. Department of Health and Human Services, 1980a.

———. *Report of the Interagency Working Group on Nitrite Research.* Washington, D.C.: U.S Department of Health and Human Services, 1980b.

——— and the U.S. Department of Agriculture. "FDA's and USDA's Action Regarding Nitrite." Draft Report, August 1978.

U.S. Office of Technology Assessment. *Cancer Testing Technology and Saccharin.* Washington, D.C.: Government Printing Office, 1977.

———. *Drugs in Livestock Feed.* Vol. 1: *Technical Report.* Washington, D.C.: Government Printing Office, 1979a.

———. *The Implications of Cost-Effectiveness Analysis of Medical Technology, Background Paper 1: Methodological Issues and Literature Review.* Washington, D.C.: Government Printing Office, 1980.

———. *Technology Assessment of Changes in the Future Use and Characteristics of the Automobile Transportation System.* Vol. 2: *Technical Report.* Washington, D.C.: Government Printing Office, 1979b.

Upton, Arthur C., Director of the National Cancer Institute, Memorandum to Commissioner, Food and Drug Administration, "Quantitative Risk Assessment," April 5, 1979.

van Rensburg, S. J. "Role of Epidemiology in Elucidation of Mycotoxin Health Risks," in J. V. Rodricks, C. W. Hesseltine, and M. A. Mehlman, eds. *Mycotoxins in Human and Animal Health.* Park Forest South, Ill.: Pathotox Publishers, 1977.

———, and others. "Primary Liver Cancer and Aflatoxin in a High Cancer Area," *South African Medical Journal,* vol. 48 (December 1974).

Watrous, R. M., and R. T. Olsen. "Diethylstilbestrol Absorption in Industry: A Test for Early Detection as an Aid in Prevention," *American Industrial Hygiene Association Journal,* vol. 20 (December 1959).

Weidenbaum, Murray L., and Robert DeFina. "The Cost of Federal Regulation of Economic Activity." American Enterprise Institute for Public Policy Research Monograph 88. Washington, D.C.: AEI, May 1978.

Weinhouse, S. "Problems in the Assessment of Human Risk of Carcinogenesis by Chemicals," in Howard H. Hiatt, James D. Watson, and Jay A. Winston, eds. *Origins of Human Cancer.* Cold Spring Harbor, N.Y.: Cold Spring Harbor Laboratory, 1977.

Weisburger, J. H., L. A. Cohen, and E. L. Wynder. "On the Etiology and Metabolic Epidemiology of the Main Human Cancers," in U.S. Congress. Senate. Committee on Agriculture, Nutrition, and Forestry. Subcommittee on Agricultural Research and General Legislation. *Food Safety and Quality:*

Nitrites. Hearings. 95 Cong. 2 sess. Washington, D.C.: Government Printing Office, 1978.

Weisburger, John H., and Charles Arnold. "Dietary Risk Factors in Cardiovascular Disease and Cancer," in U.S. Congress. Senate. Committee on Agriculture, Nutrition, and Forestry. Subcommittee on Agricultural Research and General Legislation. *Food Safety and Quality: Nitrites.* Hearings. 95 Cong. 2 sess. Washington, D.C.: Government Printing Office, 1978.

Weiss, Noel S. and Tom A. Sayvetz. "Incidence of Endometrial Cancer in Relation to the Use of Oral Contraceptives," *New England Journal of Medicine,* vol. 306 (March 6, 1980).

————, Daniel R. Szekely, and Donald F. Austin. "Increasing Incidence of Endometrial Cancer in the United States," *New England Journal of Medicine,* vol. 294 (June 3, 1976).

Weiss, William. "Smoking and Cancer: A Rebuttal," *American Journal of Public Health,* vol. 65 (September 1975).

Wennberg, John E., John P. Bunker, and Benjamin Barnes. "The Need for Assessing the Outcome of Common Medical Practices," *Annual Review of Public Health,* vol. 1 (1980).

White, Lynn, Jr. "Technology Assessment from the Stance of a Medieval Historian," *American Historical Review,* vol. 79 (February 1974).

Wilson, James Q., ed. *The Politics of Regulation.* New York: Basic Books, 1980.

Wilson, R. A., and C. M. Savage. "Restraint System Effectiveness: A Study of Fatal Accidents," in Society of Automotive Engineers, *Automotive Safety Seminar Proceedings.* Detroit: SAE, 1973.

Wilson, Richard. "Direct Testimony in the Matter of Proposed Regulations for Identification, Classification, and Regulation of Toxic Substances Posing a Potential Occupational Carcinogenic Risk. Occupational Safety and Health Administration, Docket No. 4-090 (1978)

————. "Direct Testimony: Proposed Standards for Occupational Exposure to Benzene." Occupational Safety and Health Administration, Docket No. 77H-059 (1977).

Wogan, Gerald N. "Mycotoxins and Other Naturally Occurring Carcinogens," in H. F. Kraybill and Myron A. Mehlman, eds. *Advances in Modern Toxicology.* Vol. 3: *Environmental Cancer.* New York: Wiley, 1977.

Wolf, I. A., and A. E. Wasserman. "Nitrates, Nitrites, and Nitrosamines," *Science,* vol. 177 (July 1972).

Wynder, Ernst L. "The Dietary Environment and Cancer," *Journal of the American Dietetic Association,* vol. 71 (October 1977).

————, and Steven D. Stellman. "Artificial Sweetener Use and Bladder Cancer: A Case Control Study," *Science,* vol. 207 (March 14, 1980).

Zeckhauser, R. A., and others, eds. *Benefit-Cost and Policy Analysis, 1974.* Chicago: Aldine, 1975.

Zeckhauser, Richard, and Albert Nichols. "The Occupational Safety and

Health Administration: An Overview," in *Study on Federal Regulation.* Vol. 6: *Framework for Regulation.* Appendix. Senate. Committee on Governmental Affairs. 96 Cong. 1 sess. Washington, D.C.: Government Printing Office, 1978.

Zimmerman, Burke K. "Risk-Benefit Analysis: The Cop-Out of Governmental Regulation," *Trial,* vol. 14 (February 1978).

B. Subject Listing

CASE STUDIES

Aflatoxin
Council for Agricultural Science and Technology (1979)
National Academy of Sciences (1979)
Peers and Linsell (1973)
Shank (1977)
U.S. Department of Health, Education, and Welfare (1978)
van Rensburg (1977)
———— (1974)
Wogan (1977)

Air Pollution
Barrett and Waddell (1973)
Brookshire, Ives, and Schulze (n.d.)
Crocker and others (1979)
Lave and Seskin (1977)
———— (1979)
Rowe, d'Arge, and Brookshire (1980)
Stocks (1967)
U.S. Department of Energy (1980)
U.S. Environmental Protection Agency (1979b)

Air Transportation
Keeler (1978)
National Safety Council (1980)
U.S. Department of Transportation (1975)
———— (1978)
U.S. Office of Technology Assessment (1979b)

Auto Transportation
Huelke and others (1979)
Lave (forthcoming)
———— and Weber (1970)
National Safety Council (1980)
Stowell and Bryant (1978)
U.S. Department of Transportation (1978)
Wilson and Savage (1973)

Benzene
Bartman (1980)

U.S. Environmental Protection Agency (1978)
———— (1979a)
Wilson (1977)

Carcinogens
Armitage and Doll (1961)
Higgins (1976)
Hoel (1974)
Interagency Regulatory Liaison Group (1979)
Jones and Grendon (1975)
Kendall and Kriebe (1978)
Kraybill (1977)
Lassiter (1977)
Mantel and Bryan (1960)
———— and others (1975)
Radomski (1979)
U.S. Office of Technology Assessment (1977)
Weinhouse (1977)
Weisburger, Cohen, and Wynder (1978)
Wynder (1977)

Coke Ovens
Briggs and Lave (1980)
Land (1976)
Lloyd (1970)
———— (1971)
———— and Ciocco (1969)
Mazumdar and Redmond (1979)
Miller (1976)
Redmond (1972)
———— and others (1969)
Reid and Buck (1956)
Robinson (1969)

Consumer Products
Abelson (1978)
Blum and Ames (1977)
Harris (1977)
Lenard (1979)
Merrill (1980)
National Academy of Engineers (1972)
Prunella (n.d.)

Cotton Dust
Council on Wage and Price Stability
(1977)
Crandall and Lave (forthcoming)

Diethylstilbestrol
Antonioli, Burke, and Friedman (1980)
Bailar and Byar (1970)
Barnes and others (1980)
Bibbo (1977)
———— and others (1977)
Booth (1977)
Bulow and others (1973)
Chrisman (1974)
———— and Hinkel (1974)
Council for Agricultural Science and
Technology (1977)
Crump (1978)
Cutler and others (1972)
Fitzsimons (1944)
Gass (1965)
———— (1975)
Gill, Schumacher, and Bibbo (1976)
Goldzieher and Goldzieher (1949)
Headley (1978)
Heinonen (1973)
———— (1977)
Herbst (1976)
———— and others (1974)
———— and others (1977)
————, Scully, and Robby (1975)
Hertz (1958)
———— (1977)
Huggins and Hodges (1941)
Jensen (1977)
Jones and Grendon (1975)
Jukes (1976)
Kennedy (1969)
Kliman (1977)
Kuchera (1974)
Levy (1977)
McCarrol and others (1975)
McLachlan and Dixon (1978)
Morrell and Truelove (1962)
National Academy of Sciences (1979)
Noller and Fish (1974)
Ogilvie and others (1960)
Pagani (1953)
Rumsey and others (1975)
Sheeler (1977)
Shellenberger (1979)
U.S. Department of Health, Education,
and Welfare (1977)
U.S. Office of Technology Assessment
(1979a)
Watrous and Olsen (1959)

Weiss and Sayvetz (1980)
————, Szekely, and Austin (1976)

Environment, General
Ackerman and others (1974)
Freeman (1979)
Kneese and Bower (1979)
Kraybill (1977)
Lave (1972)
———— and Silverman (1976)
Merrill (1980)
Morgan, Henrion, and Morris (1979)
National Academy of Sciences (1975)
Ruff (1978)
U.S. Department of Health, Education,
and Welfare (1977)

Food Additives, General
Hutt (1978)
Merrill (1978)

Health
Beauchamp (1980)
Belloc (1973)
———— and Breslow (1972)
Bevan (1980)
Breslow and Enstrom (1980)
Bunker, Barnes, and Mosteller (1977)
Fuchs (1974)
———— (1979)
Holtzman, Meek, and Mellits (1974)
Lave and Lave (1979)
———— and others (1976)
Omenn and Friedman (1980)
Rice, Feldman, and White (1976)
———— and Hodgson (1980)
Sackett (1975)
Starfield and Holtzman (1975)
U.S. Department of Health, Education,
and Welfare (1977)
U.S. Office of Technology Assessment
(1980)
Weisburger and Arnold (1978)
Wennberg, Bunker, and Barnes (1980)

Ionizing Radiation
Cohen (1979)
Mancuso, Stewart, and Kneale (1977)
Marnicio (1980)
National Academy of Sciences (1979a)
———— (1980)
Raabe, Book, and Parks (1980)
Terrill (1972)

Nitrites
American Meat Institute (1977)
———— (1978a)
———— (1978b)
Comptroller General of the United
States (1980)

Council for Agricultural Science and
Technology (1978)
Fassett (1973)
Fine and others (1975)
Green (1978)
Harvey and others (1976)
Ivey and others (1978)
J. C. Bard and Oscar Meyer and Com-
pany (1977)
Lijinsky (1977)
――― (1978)
――― (1979)
Magee, Montesano, and Preussmann
(1976)
Mirvish (1975)
National Academy of Sciences (1978a)
Newberne (1978)
――― (1979)
Preussmann and others (1976)
Shank and Newberne (1976)
Smith (1980)
Tannenbaum (1979)
――― and others (1978a)
――― (1978b)
U.S. Congress, Senate (1978)
U.S. Food and Drug Administration
(1980a)
――― (1980b)
――― and U.S. Department of
Agriculture (1978)
U.S. Department of Health, Education,
and Welfare (1977)
Weisburger and Arnold (1978)
―――, Cohen, and Wynder (1978)
Wolf and Wasserman (1972)

Occupational Health, General
Doniger (1978)
Freeburg (1980)
Lassiter (1977)
Merrill (1980)
National Academy of Sciences (1976)

Selikoff, Hammond, and Churq (1968)
Thaler and Rosen (1976)
Zeckhauser and Nichols (1978)

Occupational Safety
Diesler (1980)
Mendeloff (1976)
Smith (1976)
――― (1976)
U.S. Department of Labor (1979)

Photochemical Oxidants
Council on Wage and Price Stability
(1978)
Delucia and Adams (1977)
Goldstein (1980)
Marraro (1980)
Schoettlin and Landau (1961)

Saccharin
Armstrong and others (1976)
Crandall and Lave (forthcoming)
Hoover (1980)
――― and others (1979)
Kessler (1970)
Morrison and Buring (1980)
National Academy of Sciences (1978)
――― (1979c)
U.S. Office of Technology Assessment
(1977)
Wynder and Stellman (1980)

Sulfur Oxides
Comar (1979)
Crandall and Lave (forthcoming)
Holland and others (1979)
Lave and Seskin (1977)
Lipfert (1980)
Martin (1964)
Morgan and others (1978)
National Academy of Sciences (1978c)
Thibodeau, Reed, and Bishop (1980)
Water
Crandall and Lave (forthcoming)
Peskin and Seskin (1975)

FRAMEWORKS FOR REGULATION

Cost-Benefit Analysis
Baram (1979)
Dasgupta and Pierce (1972)
Debreu (1959)
DeMuth (1980a)
Harberger and others (1972)
Haveman and others (1974)
Lave (1972)
――― and Seskin (1977)
――― and Weber (1970)
Mishan (1976)

Niskanen and others (1973)
Peskin and Seskin (1975)
Prunella (n.d.)
Starr (1971)
Terrill (1972)
Zeckhauser and others (1975)
Cost-Effectiveness
DeMuth (1980a)
Hitch and McKean (1960)
U.S. Office of Technology Assessment
(1980)

General Discussions
Arrow and Hahn (1971)
Arthur Anderson and Company (1979)
Baram (1979)
Clark and Van Horn (1978)
DeMuth (1980a)
———— (1980b)
Lave (1980)
National Academy of Sciences (1975)
———— (1978b)
———— (1979c)
Noll (1971)
Rowe (1977)
Schwing (1978)
———— and Albers (1980)
U.S. Congress, House (1976)
U.S. Department of Commerce (1979)
Weidenbaum and DeFina (1978)
Wilson (1978)
Zimmerman (1967)

Market Regulation
Arthur Anderson and Company (1979)
Baram (1980)
Friedman (1962)
Galbraith (1973)
———— (1979)
Heilbroner (1965)

Keeler (1978)
MacAvoy and Snow (1977)
Mitchell (1979)
Stigler (1945)
Weidenbaum and DeFina (1978)

No-Risk
Hutt (1978)
Merrill (1978)

Regulatory Budget
DeMuth (1980a)
———— (1980b)
Nordhaus and Litan (1981)
U.S. Department of Commerce (1979)

Risk-Benefit
Clark and Van Horn (1978)
Fischoff and others (1980)
Starr (1969)
Zimmerman (1967)

Risk-Risk
Green (1978)
Leontief (1966)
U.S. Department of Commerce (1974)
U.S. Department of Labor (1978)
———— (1979)

Technology-Based Standards
Ruff (1978)

QUANTIFICATION

Aggregation of Health Effects
Berg (1973)
Brook and others (1979)
Lave and Seskin (1977)
———— and Weber (1970)
Patrick, Bush, and Chen (1973)
Raiffa (1968)
————, Schwartz, and Weinstein (1977)

Causation
Higgins (1976)
Lave and Seskin (1977)
———— (1979)
Simon (1954)
Sterling (1966)
———— (1975)
Weiss (1975)

Extrapolation of Risks
Armitage and Doll (1961)
Crandall and Lave (forthcoming)
Crump (1978)
Gaylor and Shapiro (1979)
Gori (1980)
Higgins (1976)
Hoel (1974)
———— (1975)

———— (1976)
Interagency Regulatory Liaison Group (1979)
Jones and Grendon (1975)
Kendall and Kriebe (1978)
Mantel and Bryan (1960)
———— and others (1975)
Mazumdar and Redmond (1979)
McLachlan and Dixon (1978)
Morgan, Henrion, and Morris (1979)
Omenn and Friedman (1980)
Raabe, Book, and Parks (1980)
Radomski (1979)
Rai and Van Ryzin (1979)
Upton (1979)
Weinhouse (1977)

Risk
Comar (1979)
Fischoff and others (1980)
Gori (1980)
Interagency Regulatory Liaison Group (1979)
Jones and Grendon (1975)
Kendall and Kriebe (1978)
Lowrance (1976)
Morgan, Henrion, and Morris (1979)

Morgan and others (1978)
Omenn and Friedman (1980)
Raabe, Book, and Parks (1980)
Radomski (1979)
Rai and Van Ryzin (1979)
Rowe (1977)
Schwing and Albers (1980)
Sterling (1966)
——— (1975)
Upton (1979)
Weiss (1975)

Social Discount Rate
Baumol (1968)
Denison (1979)
Epple and Lave (1980)
National Academy of Sciences (1978d)
——— (1979d)

Uncertainty
Arrow (1974)
Crandall and Lave (forthcoming)
Dreze (1974)
Epple and Lave (1980)

National Academy of Sciences (1975)
Omenn and Friedman (1980)
Raiffa (1968)
———, Schwartz, and Weinstein (1977)
White (1974)

Value of Nontraded Goods
Arrow and Kurz (1970)
Brookshire, Ives, and Schulze (n.d.)
Cohen (1979)
Cooper and Rice (1976)
Freeman (1979)
Lave (1972)
——— and Seskin (1977)
Linnerooth (1979)
National Academy of Sciences (1975)
Rice and Hodgson (1980)
———, Feldman, and White (1976)
Rowe, d'Arge, and Brookshire (1980)
Schelling (1968)
Schwing (1978)
Terrill (1972)
Thaler and Rosen (1976)

Index